A Note from the Editor

You are about to take a journey backward in time. Your means of transportation will be the written word and some glorious photographs. Your journey will take you, decade by decade, through the 20th century . . . our century.

Many of the events described in each issue of *Our Century* are famous. Some have perhaps been forgotten. Many of the people were extraordinary, some merely ordinary, a few certainly evil. All of these events and people have one thing in common, however: They have made this century a fascinating and momentous one.

All of us who worked on *Our Century* hope you find your journey into the past interesting and educational. Most of all, we hope you enjoy these "snapshots in time" as much as we enjoyed recapturing them for you.

Tony Napoli

Tony Napoli, Editor-in-Chief, *Our Century*

Statistics 1980 1990

	1980	1990
Population of the United States	226.5 million	248.7 million
Number of states in the United States	50	50
Population by race:		
White	194.8 million	208.9 million
Black	26.6 million	30.6 million
Other	5.1 million	9.2 million
Population by sex:		
Male	110 million	121.4 million
Female	116.5 million	127.3 million
Population per square mile	64.0	69.5
Life Expectancy:		
Male	70.7	72.0
Female	78.1	78.8
Number of homicides	24,278	23,440
Number of daily newspapers	1,775	1,611
Number of movie theaters	18,000	23,000
Number of households with TV sets	76.3 million	93.1 million
Number of cable television subscribers	15.5 million	47.8 million
Number of households with VCRs	1.1 million	63 million
Number of households with computers	325,000	22.5 million
Unemployment rate	6.9%	5.5%
Minimum wage	$3.10	$3.80
Children living with two parents	76.7%	72.5%
Best selling car in U.S.	Chevrolet Citation	Honda Accord
Tuition per year to a 4-year university:		
Public	$840	$2,006
Private	$3,811	$10,400
U.S. nuclear weapons tests	('70–'79) 190	('80–'89) 160
U.S. Army active-duty personnel	772,661	746,220
Prices:		
Dozen eggs	72¢	92¢
Quart of milk	41¢	83¢
Loaf of bread	36¢	$1.49
Pound of butter	$1.01	$1.39
Pound of coffee	$1.09	$3.50
Dozen oranges	96¢	$1.65

OUR CENTURY

For a free color catalog describing Gareth Stevens's list
of high-quality children's books, call 1-800-341-3569
(USA) or 1-800-461-9120 (Canada).

ISBN 0-8368-1040-6

This North American edition published by
Gareth Stevens Publishing
1555 North RiverCenter Drive, Suite 201
Milwaukee, Wisconsin 53212, USA

This edition first published in 1993 by Gareth Stevens,
Inc. Originally published in 1989 by Fearon Education,
500 Harbor Boulevard, Belmont, California, 94002, with ©
1989 by Fearon Education. End matter © 1993 by Gareth
Stevens, Inc.

Printed in the United States of America

1 2 3 4 5 6 7 8 9 98 97 96 95 94 93

Photographs: UPI/Bettmann—Cover (Sally Ride, Jesse Jackson), pp. 4, 6-8, 10, 12, 17, 22, 24, 32-43, 45-52,
54-56, 58, 59, 61, 62; Reuters/Bettmann—Cover (Reagan and Gorbachev, Joe Montana, anti-apartheid
demonstration, Tiananmen Square demonstration), pp. 11, 14-16, 18-20, 23, 25-31, 53, 57, 60, 63; The
Bettmann Archive—p. 5, 44; AP/Wide World Photos—p. 9. Advertisements: Zenith Electronics Corp., inside
front cover; Saatchi & Saatchi DFS, back cover.

1980–1990

Gareth Stevens Publishing
MILWAUKEE

Despite ERA Failure
Women in the Eighties Break Down Barriers

By the early 1980s, women in America had made much progress toward gaining equal rights with men. On June 30, 1982, however, the women's movement suffered a crushing defeat. The controversial Equal Rights Amendment (ERA) failed to become law. This proposed amendment to the U.S. Constitu-tion would have outlawed all discrimination based on sex.

The U.S. Senate had approved the amendment in 1972. Had the ERA passed, it would have been the Constitu-tion's 27th amendment. Despite a ten-year campaign by women's and civil-rights organizations, the ERA was passed by only 35 states. It fell just three states short of being ratified.

Although the ERA failed to become law, women continued to make gains during the eighties. They moved into the work force in larger numbers than ever before. By the middle of the decade, about 50 percent of all American women worked outside the home. Of course, many of these women entered the labor force out of economic necessity, and not just to get out of the house.

Jobs were once described as "women's work" and "men's work." Help-wanted ads actually said "employment for women" or "employment for men." In the 1980s, the dividing lines were fading. Growing numbers of women moved into jobs once held only by men.

Few women had ever held top positions in politics and law. During the eighties, how-ever, some of the barriers came down. In 1981, Sandra Day O'Connor was appointed the first woman justice to the U.S. Supreme Court. In 1984, Eliza-beth Dole became the first woman to head the U.S. Depart-ment of Transportation. That same year, the Democrats made a historic breakthrough by nom-inating Geraldine Ferraro as their candidate for vice presi-dent of the United States.

In 1983, Sally Ride became the first American woman to travel in space.

More women entered the work force during the 1980s than at any other time in American history.

Ferraro was the first female vice-presidential nominee of a major U.S. political party.

During the eighties, women also became U.S. space explorers. In 1983, Dr. Sally Ride became the first American woman to travel into space. In 1984, Dr. Kathryn Sullivan's space walk was another first for American women. By accepting new challenges, female astronauts also accepted new risks. Tragically, Judith A. Resnik and Christa McAuliffe were killed when the U.S. Space Shuttle *Challenger* exploded after takeoff in 1986. (See story on page 44.)

Changes in the Family

The women's revolution also changed things for many families during the 1980s. Many women continued to find satisfaction as mothers and homemakers. But as more

families needed two paychecks, fewer women were able to stay at home full time. More women took their places among society's breadwinners. In 1984, only 13 percent of American families depended on the husband as their sole source of financial support.

Having an income of their own gave women new choices. They were able to leave bad marriages, live on their own, or remain single, as they chose. Women of the eighties were marrying later. They were having fewer children and waiting longer to have them.

Many women chose to have both children and a career. They had to balance the demands of both. Though husbands often helped with household chores, in most cases working women still shouldered most of the housekeeping responsibilities. Child care, too, was usually the wife's

responsibility. Juggling family and career proved difficult for many women. Still, the majority of working women reported that they would still choose to work outside the home even if they didn't have to.

Despite its many gains, the women's movement of the 1980s was not a total success. Though some barriers fell, many of them remained. Most working women still held traditionally "female" jobs, such as clerical work, retail sales, and nursing. In 1985, only 5 percent of the top business executives in the United States were female. As late as 1989, women still earned only about 65 percent as much money as men earned for the same jobs.

In 1989, the National Women's Political Caucus quite clearly described the American women's struggle for equality: "It isn't easy, but then it isn't as hard as it used to be!" ■

A Decade of Extremes
Sleeping on the Street...

Each year as winter winds begin to howl, America's growing number of homeless people look for shelter. Some curl up under bridges and overpasses. Some sleep in doorways. Many look to public agencies for help. But many facilities for the homeless are not equipped to handle the problem. In 1985, the number of homeless people in America was estimated to range from 350,000 to 3 million. Only 91,000 public shelter beds existed in the entire country. During the 1980s, the problem of homelessness in the United States became worse than at any time since the Great Depression of the 1930s.

Who are America's homeless? They are the poorest of the poor. Many have serious personal problems. Surveys show that at least one third of America's street dwellers are alcoholics or drug abusers. Some are mentally ill. During the 1980s, the government closed many of the hospitals and institutions where these people once lived. With nowhere to go and few practical living skills, the only place left for them was the street.

By the late 1980s, the types of people who were becoming homeless had begun to change. More women and children were living on the streets. Many were escaping domestic violence. Teenagers fleeing from bad home situations often banded together with other homeless youths. They formed fiercely loyal "families" on the streets of many American cities.

Americans slowly awoke to the plight of the homeless. They began to see the desperate need for medical care, for food, for the basics of life. Many people worked to convince the government to open more shelters and

The problem of America's homeless could be found in almost any major city during the 1980s—often right alongside those who were much more fortunate.

and Million-Dollar Deals on Wall Street

provide more aid. In 1986, activists went on a hunger strike in Washington D.C. to gain funds to operate a homeless shelter. In some cities the homeless themselves staged demonstrations and sit-ins asking for public assistance. Many people felt that charity wasn't enough. Solving the problem of homelessness, they believed, required treatment programs for drug and alcohol abuse as well as mental health services and job training.

At the close of the decade, the number of street people had increased in every major U.S. city. The homeless had become a visible reminder that although America was a rich nation, there were many who did not share in the wealth.

Wall Street Billionaire

Some Americans in the 1980s struggled to find shelter from the cold. Others, like Michael Milken, built tremendous fortunes for themselves. Milken, a Wall Street bond trader, was worth more than a billion dollars by the age of 40. While homeless and jobless Americans couldn't find work at even the minimum wage of around $4 an hour, Milken earned $550 million in just one year. However, Milken's spectacular rise in fortune would be followed by an equally spectacular fall.

In 1989, the federal government charged Milken with 98 counts of racketeering and securities fraud. At first, Milken claimed he was innocent. Then he made a deal with the government. He agreed to plead guilty to some of the charges in exchange for the government dropping others. In the end, Michael Milken wound up paying a record $600 million fine and was sentenced to ten years in prison.

For some Americans, Milken and his fellow Wall Street traders were heroes of the American dream. Legions of young adults were turning their energies and talents to making money, money, and more money. They donned suits, picked up briefcases, and set out into the business world. Many put off raising families. They moved to whatever part of the country offered the best opportunities.

Ambition, education, and energy enabled many Americans during the 1980s to climb the ladder of success. People set high personal goals and worked hard to reach them. But as the rich got richer, the poor also got poorer. Society made heroes out of those who powered their way to fortune, while often ignoring the heroes who were fighting to help the poor.

In this decade of extremes, thousands of Americans struck it rich and achieved the American dream. But for thousands more, life was one continuing nightmare—of hunger, poverty, and life on the streets. ■

Wall Street bond trader Michael Milken. A swift rise to the top brought him riches; a sudden fall sent him to prison.

During the 1980s, school children as young as these kindergartners were learning from computers.

VCRs and Personal Computers
Technology Revolution Hits Home

Advances in technology allowed Americans to enjoy exciting changes in the worlds of home entertainment and computers during the 1980s.

Video-cassette recorders (VCRs) provided a brand new entertainment option. These machines allowed families to tape televised programs on cassettes and then play them back at a later time. People could also rent or buy movie tapes to play in their own homes.

The earliest VCRs came out in the 1960s. At that time, they were too complex for most consumers. Then, in 1976, Sony Corporation introduced Betamax, a smaller, simpler machine that caught on with the American public. Other companies soon developed their own recorders.

VCR owners created a huge market for the sale and rental of pre-recorded video cassettes. Stores carrying new film releases and old film classics opened in big cities and small towns all across the country. A new industry had been born, and business was booming.

PCs: From Expensive Toy to Useful Tool

In the 1980s, computers moved from the business office into the home. At the end of 1979, only about 325,000 Americans owned personal computers (PCs). By 1984, the number had soared to 15 million.

The most basic home computers were designed chiefly for entertainment. They allowed operators to shoot down enemy "Space Invaders" and to make "Pac Man" gobble up ghosts. More powerful home computers accepted many different types of programs. Games, word processing, educational, and personal finance programs became available.

By the mid-1980s, students had become one of the largest groups of PC users. Households with school-age children were three times as likely to have a computer as those without them. Educational programs served as tutors to help students with individual problems. Word processors allowed students and others to edit their work quickly. By 1989, some 37 percent of high-school students surveyed said they used a computer at home.

The price tag on home computers dropped as more competitors entered the market. Personal computers were still expensive, however. Although most students had access to computers at school, higher-income families were much more likely to have them at home.

New technology made computers and their software increasingly "user friendly"— a term coined by computer companies that means easier to use. School children were introduced to computers early. This meant that future generations would be "computer literate." By the end of the decade, home computers were becoming useful tools rather than just expensive toys. ∎

Fashion

From Dress for Success to All-Purpose Sportswear

"I am a material girl," sang pop star Madonna during the 1980s. "And I live in a material world."

The 1980s was a decade of materialism. There was a lot of talk about making money, buying things, and achieving success. Fashion reflected this trend as Americans "dressed for success." Traditional, expensive-looking clothes said "I've got it made!" Men and women paid high prices for clothing with designer labels.

During the decade, women climbed higher in the business world. Many of them chose clothing that gave them a professional, business look. They topped tailored skirts with blazer jackets. A neat bow tie or a high-collared blouse completed the look. Women expected equality in the work place, and their clothes reflected their attitude.

> In some cities youngsters were mugged and beaten just for the shoes on their feet.

Parents opened their wallets wider as teenagers, too, chose expensive clothing. Young people wanted designer jeans. They wanted athletic shoes that cost well over a hundred dollars a pair. The quest for expensive sneakers sometimes got way out of hand. In some cities youngsters were mugged and beaten just for the shoes on their feet.

Sportswear to Fashion-Wear

An exercise and fitness craze turned sportswear to fashion-wear. Running shorts, leotards, basketball shoes, and jogging suits left the gym and hit the streets. People liked the clothes because they were comfortable and well-made.

Exercise wasn't the only way to shape the body. Women during the 1980s rediscovered a trick of the 1940s. Wearing shoulder pads made their hips look slimmer. Soon shoulder pads came attached to everything from evening wear to sweatshirts.

Black became an eighties color for both men and women. All-black attire could be sophisticated, serious, or sullen. Heavy-metal jewelry, chains, and studded belts added to black suggested the violence glamorized by movies and television.

By the end of the decade, America's fashion look was a mixed bag of conservative (formal-business) and casual (sporty-trashy) attire. The one constant rule seemed to be "anything goes." ∎

A fashion model displays the tailored blazer and skirt favored by many business-women during the decade.

After 444 Days
American Hostages in Iran Released

It was a crisis that had occupied the attention of Americans for more than a year. Then suddenly it was over. On the same day that a new president took office, the 52 Americans held hostage in Iran for 444 days were finally released.

The crisis began in 1979. Islamic revolutionaries took control of the Iranian government and ousted Shah Mohammed Reza Pahlavi. The shah, a strong U.S. ally, fled Iran and eventually sought medical attention in the United States. Iran's new government, headed by religious leader the Ayatollah Khomeini, demanded the shah be returned to his homeland. U.S. president Jimmy Carter refused.

The Iranians did not like Carter's answer. Anti-American feelings in Iran began to increase. In November 1979, militant students attacked the American embassy in Iran's capital, Teheran. They captured embassy staff members and U.S. Marines. The students warned that the hostages would only be freed on one condition. The shah must be returned to Iran, along with the money he had taken when he fled the country.

The United States tried to negotiate an end to the crisis. All attempts failed. President Carter then broke off diplomatic relations and announced a ban on trade. The crisis dragged on into 1980.

In April, the United States attempted a commando-type rescue mission. It failed disastrously. Military equipment broke down, and a helicopter collided with a transport plane. Eight soldiers were killed and five were injured.

In June the shah died of cancer in Egypt. The Iranian government said the shah's death would not bring the prisoners' release.

In November, Americans went to the polls to vote for president. They elected Republican candidate Ronald Reagan by a landslide margin over President Carter. Many people felt that Carter had lost the voters' confidence because he had been unable to get the hostages freed.

In the last days of the Carter presidency, some agreements had been reached with Iran. Much of the shah's wealth would be returned. Iranian money held in U.S. banks would be released. Within minutes of Reagan's inauguration on January 20, 1981, the hostages were finally freed. A 444-day nightmare for 52 Americans and their families had come to an end. ■

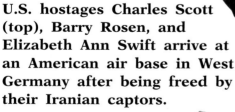

U.S. hostages Charles Scott (top), Barry Rosen, and Elizabeth Ann Swift arrive at an American air base in West Germany after being freed by their Iranian captors.

Iraq and Iran Wage Bitter War

For years the nations of Iran and Iraq had been having a dispute. Both countries wanted control of the Shatt al-Arab waterway that divided their nations. In 1980 that dispute erupted into war.

It began when Iraq's leader, Saddam Hussein, launched an attack on Iran. Hussein felt Iran had been weakened by its recent Islamic revolution. If he was expecting an easy victory, however, he turned out to be wrong.

At first there were huge land battles in which thousands of Iranians and Iraqis died. Then both sides began firing missiles at each other's major cities. Tens of thousands of civilians were killed as a result. In one horrible action, 5,000 Iraqi Kurds died when Iraqi planes dropped poison gas on an Iranian-held territory. The United Nations condemned both countries for using chemical warfare.

When attacks began on oil tankers in the Persian Gulf, the United States sent navy ships to protect the flow of oil. This led to further problems. In 1987 the USS *Stark* was hit by a missile from an Iraqi warplane. Thirty-seven Americans aboard the *Stark* were killed. Iraq apologized, calling the attack a mistake.

As the war continued, so did hostile incidents and deadly mistakes. When a U.S. vessel hit an Iranian mine, the U.S. Navy struck back. U.S. warships and planes sank or damaged six

The warship USS *Stark* sits with a gaping hole in its side after being hit by an Iraqi missile. Iraq called the attack a mistake and apologized for the incident.

Iranian ships and destroyed two oil platforms.

Tension in the Gulf led to more errors and tragedies. On July 3, 1988, a United States warship shot down an Iran Air passenger jet, killing all 290 people aboard. The U.S. cruiser *Vincennes* fired on the plane, believing it was a hostile enemy aircraft. The U.S. Navy had an explanation for the attack. It insisted that the Iranian jet was flying in a war zone. It also claimed that the plane did not follow its flight plan and did not respond to repeated radio warnings. However, President Reagan immediately said the United States regretted the attack. A week after the inci-

dent, the United States government pledged to make payments to the families of the 290 plane-crash victims.

Finally, in 1988, the United Nations arranged a cease-fire between Iran and Iraq. The eight-year war finally came to an end. It had claimed more than a million lives. The war left Iran bankrupt and Iraq $40 billion in debt. Iran had failed in its attempt to spread its brand of Islam. Iraq had gained no new territory. The two countries had been torn apart, and the United States had been drawn into a bitter conflict thousands of miles from its shores. Yet, politically, almost nothing had changed. ∎

Civil War Resumes in Lebanon

Ten years of civil war in Lebanon took a toll on innocent civilians as well as those killed in action. Here a Lebanese woman looks at the wreckage of what had once been her home.

It was a tragic, all-too-familiar story. Death and destruction on the streets of Beirut. Christians and Muslims at war with one another. Once again, as in the 1970s, civil war raged in Lebanon.

During the 1970s, the country had been torn apart by a civil war. Muslims, who made up the majority of the population, fought against Christians, who controlled most government positions. Nearly 60,000 people were killed and some $5 billion in property destroyed in just 18 months of fighting. The war ended in 1976. Saudi Arabia, and other nations in the Middle East, arranged for a cease-fire. However, the problems did not go away.

By the early 1980s, Muslims all over the Middle East were becoming more militant. Many hoped that their Islamic faith would unite the Arab world. They saw the Christian control of Lebanon as a threat to that unity. Different factions, both Christian and Muslim, formed small, private armies in Lebanon. They began fighting among themselves.

Muslim militias used brutal methods to try to drive the peacekeepers out of Lebanon.

Syria invaded Lebanon to help the Muslims. Then Palestinian fighters raided Israeli villages across the border. In return, Israel attacked the Palestinian refugee camps in Lebanon. As neighboring Middle Eastern nations were drawn into the war, U.N. peacekeeping forces entered Lebanon.

In 1982, President Reagan agreed to send U.S. troops to join the peacekeepers. At one point later that year, peace seemed possible. The troops began to withdraw. Then Israel was blamed for bombing attacks on Palestinian refugee camps. Hundreds of Palestinian civilians were killed. Tensions flared again. On September 29, President Reagan sent U.S. Marines back into Beirut.

The peacekeeping forces came under attack. In April 1983, Shiite Muslims planted a bomb in the U.S. embassy in Beirut.

The embassy was destroyed, and 87 people were killed. In October, a Muslim truck driver loaded his truck with explosives and crashed through a U.S. Marine barracks. He killed himself and 237 marines. A similar suicide mission at French military quarters left 58 dead. At home, U.S. and French citizens reacted with shock and outrage. They began to question the presence of their troops in the madhouse that Beirut had become.

Muslim militias used brutal methods to try to drive the peacekeepers out of Lebanon. They kidnapped American and European civilians. Terry Waite, a special representative of England's Archbishop of Canterbury, tried to negotiate a release of hostages. In 1987, however, he was kidnapped too. After Waite's capture, the United States ordered all American civilians to leave Lebanon.

In July 1989, Shiite Muslims showed blurry television clips of the hanging of an American hostage, Lieutenant Colonel William R. Higgins. Eight other Americans were still being held captive. The United States began to see that events had now gone beyond its control. The U.S. embassy in Beirut was ordered closed. Helicopters lifted the remaining embassy staff members to safety.

Political assassinations, terrorist bombings, and fighting between Christian and Muslim militias continued. Beirut had once been a beautiful city of high-rise buildings, hotels, and big business. Now it was in shambles. More than a decade of war had ravaged Lebanon. The fighting had involved nations halfway around the world. And the tragedy was not yet over. ∎

Muslim Minority Earns Reputation for Violence

Islam is one of the world's largest religions. People who practice Islam are called *Muslims*. Historically, most Muslims have lived in the Middle East and Indonesia. Since 1950, however, many have emigrated to Europe and North America. The great majority of Muslims are peaceful. A minority have been involved in terrorism that made the headlines during the 1980s. The violence has sometimes been wrongly associated with the whole Muslim world.

Muslims follow the teachings of their prophet, Mohammed. Mohammed was born in the Arabian city of Mecca around the year A.D. 570. It is said that when Mohammed was 40 years old, an angel spoke to him. "Teach your people that there is one God, and that God is Allah," the angel is said to have told him.

By the time Mohammed died in A.D. 632, most Arabs had become Muslims. The Islamic religion promised that followers who died battling for Allah would go straight to paradise. This idea created a huge army of enthusiastic soldiers. Muslim soldiers were ready to carry the word of Mohammed throughout the world.

From its beginning, Islam has always combined religion and politics. The Muslim ideal is a community of believers living under a single ruler according to strict Islamic law. This ideal is what radical Muslims would like to see in the Middle East. And this is what has sometimes led to great conflict.

Oil wealth and modernization have brought more and more foreign influence into the Middle East. Some small groups of Muslims feel that foreign ways threaten the Islamic religion and culture. Some of these groups hope that a revolution can create a unified Islamic state in the Middle East. Their movement is known as *Islamic resurgence*. Islamic resurgence groups consider it a religious duty to take up arms or use terrorist methods to achieve their ends.

The two major groups of Muslims are the Sunnite (*súnn-ite*) and the Shiite (*shé-ite*). The Sunnites make up more than 80 percent of the Muslim population. Most of the radicals are Shiites. Although the radical Shiites are a minority, their extreme acts keep them in the news.

The basic teachings of Islam are not about violence and terror. Islam, in fact, forbids senseless violence and urges people to battle only for just causes. In the modern world, it is only a minority of Muslims who have taken up arms. ∎

U.S.–Soviet Relations in the 1980s
Cold War Hits Deep Freeze …Then Begins to Thaw

It was a decade that began with great tension between the world's two superpowers. The United States and the Soviet Union were technically at peace. However, they found themselves in a constant "war" of harsh words.

In early 1980, the Russians referred to U.S. president Jimmy Carter as "wicked and malicious." In 1983, U.S. president Ronald Reagan called the Soviet Union the "Evil Empire." For a time it seemed as if the two nations were set on going to war with one another. But it didn't happen.

By the end of the decade, things had changed dramatically. The country's leaders stopped their name-calling. They met to talk about halting the spread of nuclear weapons. Soviet policy turned from militarism and repression toward a freer and more open society. Finally, after years of "cold war," the two superpowers began to make peace during the 1980s.

In 1979, the Soviet Union was an aggressive nation that seemed intent on spreading its form of communism. When civil war threatened to topple the pro-Soviet government in neighboring Afghanistan, Russian troops invaded the country.

The Soviet-supported Afghan government had been challenged by a Muslim resistance group. This group, the *Mujaheddin*, believed it was fighting a holy war for freedom. The Soviet troops were sent in to help the Afghan government forces.

Fighting between the Soviet troops and the *Mujaheddin* continued into the new decade.

The United States said the Soviets were wrong to send their troops into another country. In protest of the invasion, President Carter announced an embargo on U.S. grain shipments to the Soviet Union. This meant that no American grain would be delivered to the Soviet Union. Carter also banned Russian fishing off the U.S. coast. Then he canceled the export of high-technology equip-

Afghan rebels took to the mountains to fight off invading troops from the Soviet Union in 1979.

U.S. president Reagan and Soviet leader Gorbachev appeared grim as they left their summit in Iceland in October 1986. They failed to reach any agreement in reducing nuclear arms.

ment to the USSR. In addition, the United Nations General Assembly demanded that Soviet troops withdraw from Afghanistan.

The Soviets ignored these demands and refused to withdraw. In further protest, the United States and 50 other nations boycotted the 1980 Summer Olympics held in Moscow. The Soviets won 80 gold medals in those summer games. However, the absence of those other nations caused the Olympics to become a bitter reminder of the cold war.

In 1981, Ronald Reagan became president of the United States. He, too, looked coldly upon the Soviet Union and Communist aggression. President Reagan took a firm stand against the Soviets. He told Americans that it would be dangerous to appear weak. He called Soviet communism "evil in the modern world." Reagan did lift the embargo on grain sales. However, he made sure that the ban on shipments of high-technology products and the restrictions on Soviet fishing remained in effect.

President Reagan had proposed building a missile shield system in space to protect the United States against Soviet attack. The system would shoot down missiles before they could strike American land. This anti-missile system would mean a budget increase of about $1 billion a year. Reagan's anti-missile plan was nicknamed "Star Wars." Many Americans were in favor of Reagan's plan. They thought the president was right when he said that "we must find peace through strength." Others believed that the only way to achieve peace was to continue arms-limitation talks. They believed the superpowers needed to *cut* the budgets for nuclear weapons rather than increase them.

Soviets Down Korean Airliner

On September 1, 1983, a Soviet military action outraged the United States and many other nations. A Soviet fighter jet shot down a South Korean airliner carrying 269 people. Everyone aboard was killed.

The South Korean jet was flying from New York to Seoul, South Korea, when it apparently strayed off course. The airliner flew over the USSR's Sakhalin Island, off the coast of Siberia. It was an area in which Soviet military bases were located. The Soviets reported that they thought the South Korean jet was a spy plane. They said it did not respond to signals or warnings. An order was given, and the Soviet jet fired missiles at the plane. There were 61 American passengers among those killed.

"A horrifying act of violence!" declared President Reagan. The Soviets said they believed the plane was on a spying mission for the United States. They charged that the "entire responsibility for the tragedy rests with the United States." This incident made Soviet–U.S. relations colder than ever.

A New Soviet Leader

In March 1985, Mikhail Gorbachev became General Secretary of the Communist Party and

What a difference a year makes: Just 14 months after their failed summit in Iceland, Gorbachev and Reagan signed a historic nuclear treaty at the White House.

the new leader of the Soviet Union. Gorbachev was only 54. He became the youngest Soviet leader since Josef Stalin had come to power during the 1920s.

Gorbachev had new ideas. He spoke of reducing the number of Soviet nuclear weapons and of establishing more peaceful relations with the West. He promised a new spirit of *glasnost,* or openness, inside the Soviet Union. This openness would give the Russian people more freedom to express personal opinions. Gorbachev also called for *perestroika,* or reconstruction of the Soviet economy and of Soviet society. He believed that the USSR could no longer support a giant military budget and also feed its people. Gorbachev believed that the Soviet Union had to change in order to keep pace with the rest of the modern world.

The year Gorbachev came to power marked a turning point in the cold war. In November, President Reagan and the Soviet leader met in Geneva, Switzerland. The meeting was meant to provide a fresh start in U.S.–Soviet relations. Their

conversations were private, with only interpreters present. Afterwards, however, President Reagan reported that the two leaders had gotten "very friendly." Gorbachev called the meetings "productive."

Yet, while the meetings seemed friendly enough, Gorbachev told Reagan quite firmly that he wanted the U.S. "Star Wars" program abandoned. President Reagan just as firmly refused to do so. The two leaders reached no specific agreements. But at least they had shown a new willingness to work together.

Then in February 1987, Gorbachev dropped his demand that the United States limit development of its anti-missile system. In December he traveled to the United States for a historic meeting. Held in Washington D.C., it was the first meeting between Soviet and U.S. leaders on American soil since 1973. And it brought a major breakthrough.

The two superpowers signed an Intermediate Nuclear Forces (INF) treaty. This treaty called for putting an end to medium-

range nuclear missiles. Both countries would destroy all their nuclear missiles with ranges of between 300 and 3,400 miles. The United States pledged to destroy 358 missiles it had based in Europe. In return, the Soviets agreed to destroy 573 of their missiles. The nuclear threat that had been building at breakneck speed seemed at last to be coming to a halt.

Soviet Union Opens Up

The year 1988 brought further signs that US–USSR relations were improving. Mikhail Gorbachev announced that the Soviet Union would begin withdrawing troops from Afghanistan on May 15. The openness Gorbachev had promised was also bringing Western ideas into the Soviet Union. In April, Gorbachev invited 500 American businesspeople to the Kremlin to discuss joint business ventures. As a result, some American restaurant chains made plans to open restaurants in Moscow. A month later, President Reagan made his first visit to the Soviet Union.

In 1980, when Ronald Reagan was elected president, the cold war seemed to have entered a new "deep-freeze" period. Few would have guessed that before the 1980s ended, Reagan would be visiting Moscow. The president's trip was another step on the road to a U.S.–Soviet friendship. It brought Reagan to the heart of what he had called the "evil empire" just a few years earlier.

Soviet Leader Welcomed in Big Apple

Gorbachev made a return trip to the United States in December 1988. When he visited New York, thousands of people cheered him as he stepped from his limousine. Banners welcomed the Soviet leader and linked his name with peace. Americans appreciated his role in helping to end the cold war.

In 1989, the Soviet Union held its first free elections since 1917.

Gorbachev spoke to the United Nations General Assembly. He announced plans to reduce Soviet troop strength throughout Eastern Europe. He also called for an end to the idea of a Communist-versus-capitalist struggle.

Boris Yeltsin, a one-time Gorbachev supporter, resigned from the Communist Party in 1990. He called for more rapid change inside the Soviet Union.

Gorbachev's visit to New York was cut short suddenly. The Soviet leader had to return home when a disastrous earthquake struck Soviet Armenia. The quake killed over 25,000 people and left hundreds of thousands homeless. Under the new policy of *glasnost*, Soviet television reported the disaster immediately. Pictures were shown throughout the world. Western nations quickly sent aid. For the first time since World War II, the Soviets accepted American assistance.

Soviets Show "New Thinking"

In 1989, the Soviet Union held its first free elections since 1917. Citizens elected members of a new national congress. One of the candidates, Boris Yeltsin, won a landslide victory over an opponent backed by the Communist Party. Although Yeltsin himself was a party member, he had strongly criticized Gorbachev's policies. He believed Soviet reforms should come quickly, while Gorbachev had warned that change must be gradual. In 1990, Boris Yeltsin would resign from the Communist Party.

At the same time, Mikhail Gorbachev took his spirit of reform abroad. He was welcomed warmly in Great Britain and in West Germany, and he was cheered by pro-democracy demonstrators in China. The new U.S. president, George Bush, remained somewhat cautious in his view of Gorbachev's new policies. He claimed that he wanted to see if reforms would really take place. However, Bush admitted that Gorbachev's policies showed "new thinking."

The new thinking spread throughout Eastern Europe, too. Nations that had been dominated by the Soviets, such as East Germany, Hungary, and Czechoslovakia, broke ties with the USSR. They turned toward democracy. In the past, Soviet troops might have invaded these countries to keep them tied to communism. Now the tide of reform swept unchecked through these countries. By the end of the decade, Soviet foreign minister Eduard Shevardnadze had declared, "The cold war is over!" ∎

Worldwide Terrorism Brings Fear to Travelers

The acts had begun during the 1970s. Armed hijackers take over an airplane. They threaten to kill everyone on board if their demands aren't met. A radical group sets off a bomb or begins shooting people at an airport. Dozens of innocent bystanders are killed or badly injured.

At first, these acts of terrorism were rare. During the 1980s, however, they became more and more common. Throughout the decade, they caused fear and anger in travelers around the globe.

Jet Hijacked Over Greece

One of the most dramatic terrorist acts of the decade was the hijacking of a U.S. airplane on June 14, 1985. TWA Flight 847 took off from Athens, Greece, with 153 people on board. It was heading for Rome, Italy. Shortly after takeoff, two armed men seized control and forced the jet to land at the airport in Beirut, Lebanon. The hijackers announced that they were members of the group *Islamic Jihad* (holy war). They demanded that Israel release 766 prisoners, mostly Shiite Muslims.

In Beirut, the hijackers were joined on the plane by members of a Shiite militia. Then the hijackers forced the plane to fly back and forth from Beirut to Algiers four times. Between these flights, they released some of the hostages. However, the hijackers also killed one American passenger and still held 39 other American men captive in Beirut.

Neither the United States nor Israel wanted to give in to this terrorism. They refused to bargain. Then on June 24, Israel made a move that some saw as giving in to the hijackers' demands. The Israelis released 31 Shiite prisoners. Both Israel and the United States insisted that the release was not connected to the hijacking. On June 30, the remainder of the hostages from Flight 847 were set free, unharmed.

Kidnapping on the High Seas

Terrorists struck again later that same year—this time on the high seas. On October 7, 1985, four armed men seized the *Achille Lauro,* an Italian cruise ship, as it sailed off the coast of Egypt. The gunmen were members of the Palestine Liberation Front (PLF), a branch of the Palestine Liberation Organization (PLO). They threatened to blow up the ship and its 400 passengers unless Israel agreed to release 50 PLO prisoners. To emphasize their demands, the terrorists killed one passenger. The victim was 69-year-old Leon Klinghoffer, a Jewish American tourist confined to a wheelchair. After murdering this innocent man, the terrorists threw his body into the sea.

On October 9, Egypt announced that the hijackers had given up and would be turned

In 1985, terrorists held a hijacked TWA jet for more than two weeks. One passenger was killed, but the rest were finally released unharmed.

A police officer gets a first-hand look at the wreckage of Pan Am Flight 103, which exploded over Lockerbie, Scotland, in 1988. Terrorists were blamed for the explosion.

over to the PLO. An outraged United States demanded that the criminals be punished. On October 10, American jets intercepted the Egyptian airliner that was carrying the four terrorists to safety. The jets forced the airliner to land in Sicily, where the terrorists were then turned over to Italian authorities.

In the midst of all this terrorism, PLO leader Yasir Arafat continued to claim that the PLO wanted to negotiate for peace. The *Achille Lauro* incident did little to support his claim.

Explosion in Mid-Air

The most shocking and tragic terrorist act of the decade took place in 1988. On December 21, Pan Am Flight 103 ex-

ploded in mid-air over Scotland. The explosion killed all 259 people aboard, including 38 American students. The stricken jet rained fire as it fell on the village of Lockerbie. It fell on two rows of houses, killing 11 people on the ground.

At first, there seemed to be no apparent cause for the crash. The plane had been flying from London to New York when it simply disappeared from radar screens. Within days, British investigators announced that the jet had been blown apart by a powerful explosive device. They had found clues that a bomb had been hidden in a suitcase in the plane's luggage compartment.

It appeared that terrorists had planted the bomb aboard the plane. Many believed it to be the work of the PLO. Others

thought some pro-Iranian group was responsible. Iran's supporters were still angry at the United States for its accidental downing of an Iranian airliner over the Persian Gulf five months earlier.

Finally, a trail of evidence led to two Libyans. They were accused of smuggling the deadly suitcase aboard Flight 103. Libya denied the charges and refused to surrender the suspects. So it remained unclear how the world was going to bring the two Libyans to trial.

What was clear was that terrorists around the world showed no signs of stopping their activities. Travelers worldwide lived with an almost constant fear. They knew that at any time a senseless act of violence could turn a vacation into a nightmare—or death. ∎

Daniel Ortega became president of Nicaragua after the Sandinistas overthrew the Somoza government.

Aid to Contra Rebels

U.S. Backs Anti-Sandinista Forces in Nicaragua

In 1979, a group of rebels called *Sandinistas* seized control of the government in Nicaragua. This Communist group had been trying for years to overthrow the dictator Anastasio Somoza. The Somoza family had ruled the small Central American country since 1936. Although Somoza was a harsh ruler, he was an ally of the United States. He supported U.S. policies throughout the rest of Central America. He kept Nicaragua stable.

However, Somoza did little for the people of Nicaragua. The very rich got richer, but the millions of poor grew poorer. Somoza kept control with violence. His police force, the National Guard, fiercely put down any protest. During the late 1970s, America finally withdrew its support for the Somoza government. When the U.S. refused to send more arms to the National Guard, the Sandinistas toppled the Somoza government.

President Reagan maintained that the Sandinista regime presented a Communist threat to the Americas.

Relations between the United States and the Sandinista government were strained. The United States feared that the Sandinistas would provide a Communist stronghold in Central America. The United States accused Nicaragua of helping Communist rebels in El Salvador and of relying on Soviet aid and support.

A group known as the Contras (*contra* means "against" in Spanish) rebelled against the Sandinistas. U.S. president Ronald Reagan announced that the United States would provide aid to the Contras. Many Americans questioned this U.S. policy. They believed that the United States should not interfere with the politics of another nation. President Reagan pointed out that the Sandinistas were receiving Soviet tanks and aircraft. He continued to maintain that the Sandinista regime presented a Communist threat to the Americas.

In 1983, the U.S. House of Representatives voted to cut off aid to the Contras. However, the United States did not pull out of Nicaragua's affairs. In 1984, the U.S. Central Intelligence

Agency (CIA) admitted responsibility for setting explosive mines in Nicaraguan ports. The CIA had planned to stop any ships carrying Sandinista supplies. Nicaragua complained of outside interference to the International Court of Justice. The CIA said it would stop its activity.

The Sandinistas called the United States "aggressors." In 1986, Nicaragua shot down a U.S. cargo plane carrying supplies for the Contras. The United States said the plane was on a private mission. Nicaragua charged that the CIA was behind this delivery and other shipments of arms.

More illegal U.S. aid to the Contras came to light. In 1986, it was revealed that America had sold arms earlier to the hostile Middle Eastern nation of Iran. Profits from these secret arms sales went to the Nicaraguan Contras. Many people who

were against U.S. policy in Nicaragua condemned these secret sales. Congress held an investigation into the matter. (See story on page 41.)

In August 1989, Nicaragua took a major step toward ending the civil war. President Daniel Ortega signed a treaty with the rebels. The Contras promised to lay down their arms and refuse any further outside aid. In return, the Sandinistas said there would be no arrests of Contra members. Democratic elections were scheduled to be held the following year.

After several more months of periodic battles, elections were finally held in February 1990. In a major surprise, Violeta Barrios de Chamorro defeated Ortega. She became the new president of Nicaragua. The Nicaraguans hoped she would help heal the wounds caused by ten years of bloody civil war. ∎

Democratic elections in Nicaragua were finally held in February 1990.

U.S. Backs Government of El Salvador

The people of Nicaragua weren't the only ones engaged in a civil war in Central America during the 1980s. The nation of El Salvador was also torn by military struggle between opposing forces. This time the United States sided with the government in power.

Civil unrest had rocked El Salvador for many years. In 1979, the military took control of the government. Rebels fought against the new military rule. These rebel fighters were armed by Cuban and Nicaraguan Communists. The rebels launched guerrilla attacks on the government armies. The military fought back with toxic gases and bacterial warfare. Thousands of civilians were killed. Hundreds of thousands more fled the country to escape the violence that had become part of daily life in El Salvador.

The United States sent aid to the military government. The Reagan administration said the United States had to defend itself against Communist influences from Cuba and Nicaragua. Some Americans were opposed to this aid. They said the El Salvadoran government attacked civilian populations and ordered "death squad" assassinations.

In 1984, El Salvadoran voters turned out in large numbers to elect Jose Napoleon Duarte to the presidency. Duarte promised a more moderate, humane government. His opponents charged that he won the election with help from the U.S. government. Rebel guerrilla attacks continued throughout the decade. By 1990, the tragedy of Salvadorans killing one another had entered its tenth year. ∎

India's leader Indira Gandhi died at the hands of assassins.

Assassins Kill Indira Gandhi

S hock waves rolled through the nation of India on Oct. 31, 1984. The country's 66-year-old leader, Prime Minister Indira Gandhi, had been shot and killed by two of her own bodyguards. The murder was an act of revenge by members of the Sikh religion.

Sikh rebels had been seeking a separate state in their region of India. In June, Gandhi had ordered the capture of their headquarters at the Golden Temple in Amritsar. The temple was the holiest of Sikh shrines. Seizure of the temple angered many Sikhs and led to the murder plot.

Indira Gandhi became India's first woman prime minister in 1966. Born into a well-known Hindu family, Gandhi's childhood revolved around her country's politics. Her grandfather had been a leader in India's struggle for independence from Great Britain. Her father, Jawaharlal Nehru, had been the newly independent India's first prime minister.

Gandhi studied at Oxford University in England. She then married Feroze Gandhi (no relation to independence leader Mohandas K. Gandhi). After her marriage, Gandhi became her father's valued adviser. Follow-ing his death in 1964, she became India's minister of information and broadcasting. In 1966, Nehru's successor, Prime Minister Shastri, died. Indira Gandhi was asked to run for the office and was elected.

Indira Gandhi was a firm leader with strong ideas. She gained enormous popularity by supporting independence for East Pakistan (now Bangladesh). However, drought and inflation caused food shortages in India. Gandhi's popularity declined as economic conditions worsened.

In 1975, Indira Gandhi was accused of illegal campaigning. Many Indians demanded that she resign. Instead, she turned a strong hand against her accusers. She declared a state of emergency and arrested thousands of her opponents. She silenced her critics by taking away freedom of the press.

Despite her harsh actions, by 1977 Gandhi felt sure of her position and popularity. She called for new elections. She was surprised when she was swept out of office. However, the new government also failed to solve India's problems. In 1980, Indira Gandhi was again elected prime minister.

After Gandhi's assassination, her son Rajiv became prime minister. It became his job to heal the nation's wounds following his mother's murder.

As India's leader, Indira Gandhi had not allowed her country to be torn apart by religious differences. Her bold actions against the Sikh movement held India together. However, they also cost Indira Gandhi her life. ∎

The Long Battle Against Apartheid

The smoke of fires hung over burned-out houses. Dirt roads were quiet now, but only hours earlier the air had thundered with the shouts of protesters. Rocks had shattered windows, and police batons had battered dark bodies. Children had screamed in terror.

The place was a township outside Johannesburg, South Africa. The time was 1984. In the days following these latest riots, funerals were held for the 14 blacks who had died. Grim men and women raised their fists next to coffins draped with flags of the African National Congress (ANC). The ANC was an outlawed black political party that was leading the fight against apartheid.

This scene was a familiar one in South Africa during the 1980s. Thousands died protesting apartheid, a system that had divided the black majority from the white minority since 1948. Afrikaners, descendants of South Africa's Dutch colonists, wanted to make sure whites controlled South Africa. They separated people according to race. By law, people of certain races could live, own property, or run businesses only in certain zones.

Black South Africans were forced into crowded ghettos called townships. Curfews restricted the times when blacks could be on the streets. Separate trains, beaches, schools, and other facilities were provided for blacks and whites.

P. W. Botha was appointed president of South Africa in 1984. At the same time, a new constitution was approved. It brought a wave of demonstrations from the black majority. The new constitution gave blacks no voice at all. The demands for change soon began to look like a revolution. Government buildings were looted or set on fire. In 1986, President Botha declared a state of emergency. He set up even stricter regulations and jailed 20,000 anti-apartheid leaders and protesters.

F. W. de Klerk replaced P. W. Botha as president in August 1989. De Klerk promised that South Africa was on the "threshold of a new era." In October, he gave official permission for an anti-government demonstration. Some 20,000 protesters marched through Johannesburg calling for an end to racist rule. There was no police response.

In 1990, President de Klerk released the jailed leader of the ANC, Nelson Mandela. The 71-year-old Mandela had been in prison for 27 years. Upon his release, Mandela once again became his country's chief anti-apartheid messenger. He and his wife, Winnie, and South African clergyman Archbishop Desmond Tutu spoke in many countries on behalf of their movement. In South Africa itself, it was clear that the fight for racial justice would continue. ■

This scene was an all-too-familiar one in South Africa as many people lost their lives in the battle against apartheid.

The Philippines— Islands of Unrest

For 20 years Ferdinand Marcos was president of the island nation of the Philippines. Then in 1986, he was driven out of his country. When Marcos left his homeland, he fled to the United States. He died in exile in Honolulu, Hawaii, on September 29, 1989. Even in death, however, Marcos could not go home. The new Philippine president, Corazon Aquino, would not allow Marcos's body to be returned home for burial. The conflict between Marcos and Aquino is central to the political unrest that rocked the Philippines during the 1980s.

Ferdinand Marcos was elected president of the Philippines in 1965. Marcos was a popular, colorful figure. During World War II, he had won medals fighting to protect the Philippines from Japanese control. After the war he was elected first to the Philippine House of Representatives and then to the Senate.

As president, Marcos could not bring stability to his country. His early years in power were marred by rebel riots and Communist guerrilla attacks. In 1972 Marcos cracked down. He declared martial law. He gave his military increased power to keep control and halt rebellion. He gave himself more power to pass laws. In 1973, Marcos proclaimed a new constitution. It granted the president even more control. Marcos also gave political authority to his wife, Imelda Marcos. He put her in charge of the nation's planning and development.

The Philippines remained under Ferdinand Marcos's iron hand for more than eight years. In 1981, Marcos lifted martial law. He freed political prisoners and gave law-making powers back to the National Assembly. He was reelected to a six-year term as president.

Political Rival Assassinated

The beginning of the end for Marcos came in 1983. A Philippine politician named Benigno Aquino was a strong rival of Marcos. Aquino had lived in the United States for three years. Then, in August

Philippine president Ferdinand Marcos was forced out of power after being linked to the murder of a political rival.

1983, he returned to his country to lead the opposition against Marcos. When he arrived at the airport in Manila, Benigno Aquino was gunned down and killed.

The killer was an unknown person who could not be connected to any political group. President Marcos insisted he knew nothing about the assassination. But the murder set off anti-government riots and protests. Demonstrators linked Marcos to Aquino's murder. They demanded that the president resign.

Benigno Aquino was dead. But his widow, Corazon Aquino, took over his cause. She ran against Marcos in the February 1986 presidential election. When Marcos declared himself the winner, Aquino accused him of stealing the election. U.S. president Ronald Reagan supported Aquino and urged Marcos to resign.

Near the end of February, two of Marcos's closest advisers came forward. They said Marcos had rigged the election. They also accused Marcos of ordering the murder of Benigno Aquino.

Both Corazon Aquino and Ferdinand Marcos declared themselves to be president. On February 25, two separate ceremonies were held. In one, Aquino was sworn in as president. In the other, Marcos was sworn in. On February 26, however, Ferdinand Marcos left his country. He fled rather than face charges of murdering Benigno Aquino and of robbing the government treasury. His wife Imelda escaped with him. The United States and other nations immediately recognized Corazon Aquino as president of the Philippines.

Despite her early popularity, Aquino faced the same problems Marcos had faced. The economy was still weak. The people were

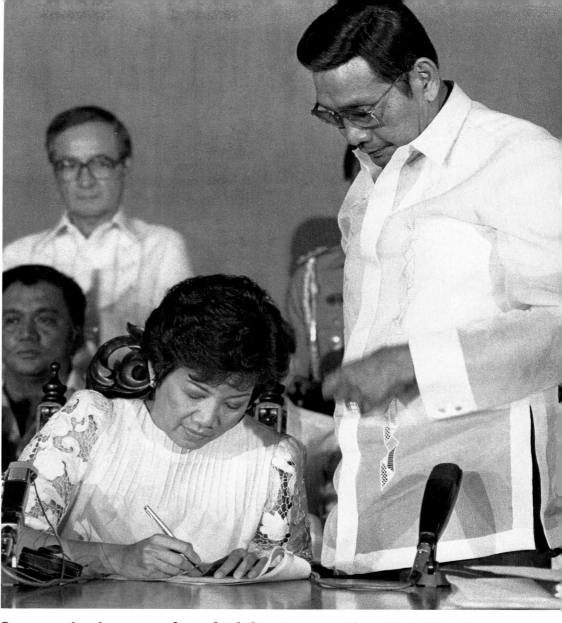

Corazon Aquino was elected Philippine president in 1986. She became leader of the opposition to Marcos after her husband Benigno Aquino was murdered.

still poor. The government seemed unable to stop a series of political murders. Communist rebels continued riots and attacks. The leadership of the Philippines had changed hands, but the atmosphere of lawlessness remained the same.

Those who were most unhappy with President Aquino were certain members of the Philippine military. They said that she was not taking strong enough action against the Communist guerrillas. Then, on November 30, 1989, rebel forces from within the Philippine military turned on Aquino. They launched an all-out effort to take over the government. They seized air force headquarters and several television stations. They attacked the presidential

palace. Bloody battles raged in the capital city of Manila. During the fighting, 79 people were killed and more than 500 were wounded.

Neither side seemed able to win until the United States stepped in. America had its own interests to protect. Treaties between the two governments allowed U.S. military bases in the Philippines. Another treaty promised mutual defense in times of need. U.S. president George Bush came to Aquino's aid. Faced with the threat of force from U.S. fighter jets, the rebel soldiers surrendered.

As 1990 began, Corazon Aquino was still in power. However, her future as leader of the Philippines was by no means secure. ∎

American Troops Go After Panama's Drug King

A storm was brewing in Panama in 1987. At its center was General Manuel Noriega, commander of the Panamanian defense forces. Panama's president was Eric Arturo Delvalle, but all the real power lay in the hands of Noriega.

It was no secret that Noriega was corrupt. Some of his own supporters accused him of smuggling drugs. They said he tampered with election votes so his candidates would win.

Noriega denied the charges against him. He blamed the United States for stirring up false rumors. Pro-Noriega demonstrations were held outside the U.S. embassy in Panama City. The protestors caused more than $100,000 worth of damage. The United States suspended all military and economic aid to Panama.

On February 5, 1989, the United States officially accused Noriega of drug smuggling. The U.S. government said Noriega's illegal activities dated back to 1981. Because of the drug charges, Panama's President Delvalle fired Noriega from his command. Noriega was too powerful, though. His troops remained loyal to him. They drove President Delvalle into hiding.

In protest of Noriega's actions, the United States froze all Panamanian assets in America. This caused a cash shortage in Panama. Banks closed, and pay was withheld from government workers.

Noriega crushed all attempts to remove him from power. The U.S. government offered Noriega a deal. If he would step down, they would drop drug charges against him. Noriega refused.

Soon a new national election was held. It seemed like the perfect time to get rid of Noriega. Indeed, his opponents did win the election. Nothing changed, however. Noriega ignored the election results. He refused to give up power.

On December 23, 1989, U.S. president George Bush sent 24,000 U.S. troops to Panama to drive Noriega from power. At an American military base Guillermo Endara, who had been rightfully elected by the Panamanian people, was sworn in as president. Then American forces attacked. For three days Panama City was in chaos. Looters and snipers ruled the streets. Finally the U.S. troops established order.

However, General Noriega had not been captured. American troops searched for him. They found illegal drugs in his office. They found $3 million in cash and a stash of weapons in his home. The general himself, however, remained at large somewhere in the countryside.

Finally, on December 29, Noriega emerged from hiding to seek protection at the Vatican embassy in Panama City. American officials negotiated with the Vatican for Noriega's release. A few days later, Noriega surrendered to the American military forces. He was then brought back to the United States to stand trial on drug charges. ■

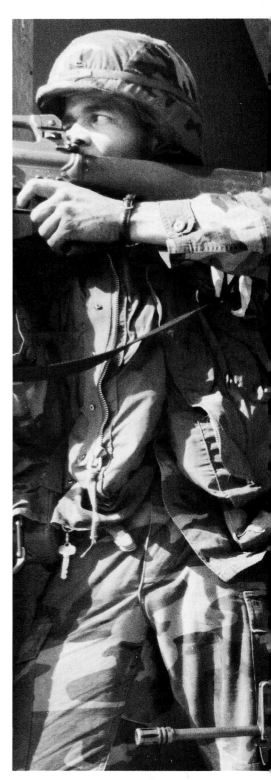

U.S. forces invaded Panama in 1989 to remove General Manuel Noriega from power.

A Ten-Year Struggle for Solidarity

Poland Throws Off Communist Rule

Food shortages, poor working conditions, and low wages had plagued Polish workers throughout the 1970s. In 1980, the workers took a stand. They wanted to form a trade union, something unheard of in Communist Eastern Europe. The workers called their union *Solidarity*. At first, angry Poles went on strike at the Lenin Shipyard in Gdansk. The strike spread to other factories, and soon more than 500,000 workers had walked off their jobs. The strikers demanded freedom of speech, the release of political prisoners, and new labor laws. A Polish shipyard worker named Lech Walesa became the leader of Solidarity.

Two months of labor strikes took a hard toll on the Polish economy. Finally, the government gave in. It granted the workers at the Gdansk shipyard the right to form independent trade unions. This was a dramatic, first-time event in a Communist nation.

More strikes took place, and Solidarity brought gains for Polish workers. Then, in 1981, General Wojciech Jaruzelski became the new prime minister and Communist Party leader. Jaruzelski was determined to control labor unrest. He announced that he would "save" Poland from disaster and civil war. He increased the power of the Polish military. Then he banned public gatherings and demonstrations and declared Solidarity outlawed. Many workers were arrested, including Lech Walesa. The Soviet Union supported Jaruzelski's Communist regime. The United States voiced strong disapproval of Poland's military crackdown.

On May 1, 1982, some 50,000 Poles marched through the streets of Warsaw. They chanted support for Solidarity and protested military rule. The government tightened its restrictions. Sporting events were canceled, and private cars were banned from the streets. In October, the United States reacted to Poland's harsh restrictions. For 22 years, Poland had enjoyed a "most-favored nation" trade status with the United States. That meant Poland paid low charges on goods that it exported to the United States. President Reagan took that status away. This strained Poland's economic conditions even more.

The Polish government was finally forced to give in. In November 1982, Lech Walesa was released from prison. His efforts and those of Solidarity were recognized in 1983 when Walesa was awarded the Nobel Peace Prize.

During the mid-1980s, economic conditions in Poland continued to worsen. Tensions between the government and workers remained high.

In 1988, there were widespread strikes by Solidarity supporters. For the first time since 1981, the Polish government held talks with Walesa and other Solidarity leaders.

By 1989, Polish leaders were ready to change. They made Solidarity legal again. The union formed its own political party. In the next election, a majority of its leaders were elected to the Polish National Assembly. In 1990, Lech Walesa was elected president of Poland. For the first time in 40 years, Poland would have a government led by non-Communists. ∎

From prisoner to president: Solidarity leader Lech Walesa was arrested by the Polish Communist government in 1981. By 1990, Walesa had been elected president.

In November 1989, thousands of Czech citizens filled Prague's Wenceslas Square to call for democracy. Within the month, the Communist government was forced to give up power.

Winds of Change Sweep Across Eastern Europe

It had taken ten years for the citizens of Poland to free themselves from Communist rule. In other parts of Eastern Europe, however, the changeover happened at nearly lightning speed—taking less than ten *months*.

In earlier decades, some Soviet-controlled nations had tried to break ties with the USSR. In 1956, Soviet troops crushed a Hungarian movement for independence. In 1968, Soviet tanks rumbled into Czechoslovakia to maintain control of that government. By 1989, however, the Soviets no longer had a stranglehold on Eastern Europe. With this new freedom some Eastern European nations turned to more democratic governments.

In 1989, Hungary became the first Soviet-bloc nation to give up communism. In May of that year, Hungary had opened up its border with Austria, its free neighbor to the west. By late summer, the government was allowing thousands of East Germans in Hungary to flee to freedom in the West. The action was taken despite the objections of East Germany. This move by the Hungarian government tore a large hole in the "Iron Curtain" that had been "draped" across Eastern Europe since World War II.

In October, tens of thousands of Hungarians jammed Republic Square in Budapest. They came to hear their country officially declared a free republic. A multi-party government was established. Then, in November, the country held its first free elections since the end of World War II.

Throughout much of 1989, citizens of Czechoslovakia held peaceful demonstrations calling for freedom and change. At first, these demonstrations were put down forcefully by Czech police. The cries for reform continued, however, and the number of supporters grew. In November, the police broke up one large demonstration by severely beating a number of the student protesters. This only further angered the Czech people.

The major Czech opposition group called itself the Civic Forum. In late November, government leaders agreed to meet with Civic Forum leader Vaclav Havel to discuss new freedoms. But the strikes and demonstrations continued. Communist leaders were forced to give up power. On December 29, the country's National Assembly elected Vaclav Havel president of Czechoslovakia. Free democratic elections were scheduled to be held in 1990.

The 1989 reforms swept through the Eastern European countries of Bulgaria and Yugoslavia, as well. In Bulgaria, the Union of Democratic Forces brought swift changes to the Communist government. Fifty thousand people gathered to demand that Bulgaria's Communist Party hold free elections. In Yugoslavia, the Communist Party pledged to give up its monopoly on power and to hold free elections soon. ∎

It was the single most recognized symbol of the cold war—a 26-mile-long, 15-foot-high wall. For nearly 30 years the Berlin Wall had divided the city of Berlin and the people of Germany. It had stood as a constant reminder of the lack of understanding between the free West and the Communist East. Remarkably, though, the winds of change that swept across Eastern Europe in 1989 blew that wall down.

Ever since it had been built in 1961, East Germans had been trying to cross the wall to freedom. They risked their lives to escape. Now, in 1989, freedom-seekers saw the changes happening in the Soviet Union. They saw reform in Poland and Hungary. They saw that West Germany, a democracy, had become one of the richest countries in the world. East Germans had few freedoms and were still quite poor by comparison.

In mid-September of 1989, thousands of East Germans had crossed the newly opened border from Hungary to Austria. From there they made their way to West Germany. The East German government, under mounting criticism at home, was powerless to prevent this escape.

In early November, one million East Germans rallied in East Berlin. They demanded major economic and political reforms. On November 7, the country's entire Council of Ministers—the official government—resigned.

Then, on November 9, East Germany threw open the gates of the Berlin Wall. Within hours of its opening, thousands of East Germans poured across the border. Thousands more danced for joy atop the wall. Some took up picks and shovels and began to tear the wall down. People around the world shared the East Germans' excitement. Travelers came to see the symbol of oppression fall. They took home pieces of the wall as souvenirs of freedom.

At the end of 1989, the Communists in East Germany were barely clinging to power. They changed leaders several times. They promised reforms and free elections soon. It was too little, too late, though. In 1990, East Germany held its first free elections since World War II. The Communists were voted out of office.

The new leaders of East Germany worked out a plan

The Wall Comes Tumbling Down

A young girl stands atop the rubble of what had once been part of the Berlin Wall.

with West Germany to join into a single, reunified country. Helmut Kohl was elected the first chancellor of this reunited Germany. Maps were redrawn as Germany once again became one independent nation.

Revolution in Romania

The fall of communism in Poland, Hungary, Czechoslovakia, and East Germany was accomplished with very little violence. However, in one Eastern European country, change came only through bloodshed.

For 24 years, Nicolae Ceausescu had ruled Romania with an iron fist. Romanians had none of the basic freedoms

A young man waves the Romanian flag with the Communist symbol cut out after the fall of Nicolae Ceausescu.

people in the West took for granted. Anyone who criticized the Ceausescu government was likely to be arrested, tortured, or even put to death.

Ceausescu's main concern was paying off Romania's foreign debt. He exported food to bring in money even while his people were starving. Ceausescu's own family, however, lived very well. His wife was his second in command. He gave other relatives important, high-paying government jobs. Some people said that Ceausescu himself had over $1 billion hidden away.

Ceausescu used fear to keep the Romanians in line. In the face of hunger and oppression, however, that fear eventually gave way to anger. And the anger sparked a revolution.

In December 1989, people all over Romania gathered in city squares to demonstrate against their dictator. Government troops turned on the

people. They killed thousands of unarmed men, women, and children. The long-suffering Romanians would not be stopped, however. Demonstrations continued. Many army troops began to side with the people. Finally, after several violent street battles, the revolutionaries seized control.

By year's end, Nicolae Ceausescu and his wife had been captured while trying to escape from the country. They were quickly tried for their crimes and executed. The new government removed the Communist emblem from the nation's flag and passed laws granting personal rights. It announced that free elections would be held the following spring. A hated ruler had been overthrown, but at a high cost. It was estimated that between 10,000 and 80,000 Romanians had died during the revolution in the final two weeks of December 1989. ■

In May 1989, Chinese students in Tiananmen Square called for more freedom and democracy inside their country.

Chinese Troops Kill Students

Tiananmen Square Massacre Halts Democracy Movement

Voices calling for democracy were heard briefly, but loudly, in China during 1989. Those voices were fiercely silenced by a hardline Communist government led by Deng Xiaoping.

In May 1989, Soviet president Mikhail Gorbachev visited China. The purpose of his visit was to try to end Soviet–Chinese hostilities. When the Soviet leader arrived, nearly two million demonstrators were in the streets. The demonstrators were mostly Chinese students. They were there to cheer Gorbachev's policy of openness and reform inside the Soviet Union. They demanded democracy for their own nation. At the same time, thousands of students were staging a hunger strike in Tiananmen Square, in the capital city of Beijing. The Chinese government was embarrassed by the protests. Chinese officials kept Gorbachev away from the square.

The pro-democracy movement was not limited to the capital. Hundreds of thousands of protesters rallied for freedom in other Chinese cities. In many places, protest leaders were quickly arrested. When troops were sent into Beijing to put down the demonstrations, students and workers blocked their way. Some men and women lay down in the streets to prevent tanks from passing. Protesters carried signs asking the government "not to use the People's Army against the people."

The hardline Communists, however, would not stand for the demonstrations. When students built a copy of America's famous Statue of Liberty in Tiananmen Square, they were arrested. Then tens of thousands of government troops moved in to crush the remaining demonstrators. Tanks rolled through the square, driving over automobiles and killing those still inside. Soldiers fired automatic weapons wildly into crowds of students. Leaders of the demonstrations reported that more than 2,000 people were killed. The government refused to list the casualties of the massacre.

Deng Xiaoping appeared on Chinese television after the massacre. He pictured the Tiananmen demonstrators as "thugs and hoodlums" who threatened national welfare. The government began arresting those thought to be connected with demonstrations, strikes, and protests. Hundreds of pro-democracy supporters were jailed. Some demonstration leaders were executed.

The United States and other Western nations condemned the violence in China. U.S.–Chinese relations, which had been steadily improving, took a big step backward.

The exact number of people killed that spring and summer in China may never be known. The Communists' official word was that the massacre in Tiananmen Square "never happened." Thousands of students, the government insists, were not shot. In a modern age, however, it is hard to rewrite history. Television and worldwide communications let the truth be seen, heard, and read. Democracy was brutally beaten down in China in 1989. It was beaten down by a government that was afraid of its own people. ∎

AIDS: Epidemic of the Eighties

Rallies to help stop the spread of AIDS often featured memorials to those who had died from the disease.

A killer was loose during the 1980s. It was a disease called AIDS. Scientists identified the disease in 1981 and named it acquired immune deficiency syndrome (AIDS). They discovered it was caused by a virus—the human immunodeficiency virus (HIV). This virus destroys the body's defenses against infection. They also found that this virus that causes AIDS spreads from person to person. Because of this, scientists and doctors feared there would soon be a worldwide epidemic.

Since 1981, AIDS has shown up in some 140 countries around the world. It exploded into the most widespread epidemic in central Africa. In some African cities, 15–30 percent of the adult population was reported to be infected with the virus. High numbers of AIDS cases were also found in the small Caribbean nation of Haiti. By the end of the decade, there were very few countries in which this killer disease had not struck.

The AIDS virus can be passed in only two ways: through direct blood-to-blood contact, or through an exchange of bodily fluids. One way a person can get AIDS is by having sexual intercourse with an infected person. Sometimes needles shared by drug users carry the virus. AIDS can also be passed through transfusions of infected blood. By the end of the decade, though, screening of blood donors and testing of blood supplies had nearly eliminated this problem.

In some cases, infected women pass the disease to their babies during pregnancy or childbirth. Sexual habits and drug use are subjects many people prefer not to discuss. Some people believe that years of silence allowed the AIDS virus to spread more quickly.

In the United States, the topics of AIDS education and AIDS prevention caused controversy. Some people thought the schools should take a leading role in teaching young people about AIDS. Others were uncomfortable with schools that gave out information about safe sexual practices and condoms.

Education was the key, not only to preventing AIDS, but also to protecting its victims. When the virus first appeared, many people were afraid of AIDS patients. Some worried that they could catch the virus from sitting next to or touching an infected person. In 1987, a Florida family received bomb threats when their three AIDS-infected sons tried to attend a public school. The boys had all received blood transfusions infected with the AIDS virus. The family was forced to move to another city. It was clear that the public needed to learn that AIDS could not be spread through casual contact.

At the end of the decade, the AIDS outlook was grim. No cure for the disease was in sight. The World Health Organization (WHO) estimated that by the year 2000 as many as 15 to 20 million people could be infected with the virus worldwide. ∎

Reported AIDS Cases as of 1990	
U.S., Canada	1 million
Latin America, Caribbean	more than 1 million
Western Europe	500,000
North Africa, Middle East	50,000
Sub-Saharan Africa	6.5 million
South and Southeast Asia	more than 1 million
Australasia	30,000
Eastern Europe, USSR	20,000
East Asia, Pacific Islands	20,000

Reagan Unseats Carter for Presidency

People in the huge hall cheered loudly as red, white, and blue balloons floated from the ceiling. A banner on the stage read, "Together—A New Beginning." Bands played a victory song. The site was the 1980 Republican National Convention in Detroit. And Ronald Reagan had just been named the Republican candidate for president of the United States.

Three months later, in the presidential election, Reagan buried President Jimmy Carter under a landslide of electoral votes. The 69-year-old former California governor had become the nation's 40th president. Reagan's poise and winning ways had swept him from the sound stages of Hollywood all the way to the White House.

From Actor to Politician

During the 1940s and 1950s, Ronald Reagan had been a successful motion picture and television star. In 1966, he took the charm and polish that had served him so well in show business and turned it toward politics. He was elected governor of California that year and again in 1970. He made a bid for the Republican presidential nomination in 1976 but narrowly lost to Gerald Ford. When he sought the nomination a second time in 1980, he won.

Reagan's nomination came during a troubled time. By the summer of 1980, America was moving deeper into a recession. Inflation and unemployment were rising. Foreign competition was hurting U.S. industry.

President Jimmy Carter was tackling difficult foreign matters as well. In 1979, Muslim revolutionaries had attacked the U.S. embassy in Iran and taken hostages. By the summer of 1980, some 52 Americans were still being held in that Middle Eastern nation. Reagan promised to solve many of the problems both at home and abroad.

Reagan spoke of the recession as the "Carter Depression." He proposed tax cuts to help the economy. He explained that with lower taxes, individuals and businesses would have more money to invest in American companies. Industry could produce more goods, and inflation would be halted.

Ronald Reagan waves to the crowd just before making his acceptance speech at the 1980 Republican National Convention.

President Jimmy Carter and Ronald Reagan shake hands before one of their televised debates during the 1980 campaign.

Government was too big, Reagan said, and spent too much money. As governor of California, Reagan had been known as a political conservative. He praised private enterprise and complained about government interference.

Reagan summed up his economic platform: "The way to fight inflation is to whittle down the size of the federal government," he said. "Remove the layers of fat, and then cut the income taxes across the board for everybody in the country!"

Critics wondered what all this whittling and cutting would do to social services and welfare programs. They worried that Reagan's cuts would mean disaster for poorer Americans.

While proposing slashes in government spending, Reagan refused to cut the defense budget. In fact, he wanted to increase military spending. He warned that Americans needed new weapons to keep pace with the Russians. The United States, he said, must defend against the Communist threat of the Soviet Union. With the hostage crisis in Iran, many Americans liked Reagan's bold words and fighting spirit.

The Democrats launched their own campaign. President Carter reminded voters of his achievements. During his term in office, Carter said, no American soldier had died in battle. The president described improved relations with China. He recalled the 1979 Arab–Israeli peace treaty. He pointed out how many times Reagan had favored military intervention. In a nuclear age, Carter warned, America needed a president who could show restraint.

Early surveys showed both Reagan and Carter doing well. Experts said the election was too close to call.

It was not the close election that nearly everyone had predicted. Reagan and his vice-presidential running mate, George Bush, won by a landslide. The popular vote was 51 percent for Reagan and 41 percent for Carter. But in the electoral votes by states, Ronald Reagan received 483, while Carter only got 49. Some people blamed the hostage crisis in Iran for Carter's overwhelming loss. They said it was Iran's leader, the Ayatollah Khomeini, who beat Jimmy Carter.

If Reagan's big victory was a surprise, the outcome of the congressional races was a shock. For the first time since 1952, the Republicans had won control of the Senate. The Democrats kept control of the House of Representatives, but the Republicans made gains there as well.

Some people blamed the hostage crisis in Iran for Carter's overwhelming loss.

The greatest surprises lay ahead. Would Reagan's conservative ideas boost the economy? Would hard-line foreign policy win America respect or make enemies? Would an arms build-up deepen the cold war? A new decade was dawning, and some surprising history was about to be made. ∎

A Generation Mourns John Lennon

He became famous for writing and singing songs about peace and love. He died in a mindless act of violence that shocked and saddened people throughout the world. On December 8, 1980, a 25-year-old stranger walked up to John Lennon and shot him to death outside his home in New York.

John Lennon was a singer and a poet. During the 1960s, he soared to fame as a member of the remarkable rock 'n' roll group, the Beatles. Lennon and fellow Beatle Paul McCartney became the most famous pop song-writing team of their time.

John Lennon was born on October 9, 1940, in Liverpool, England. At age 16, he formed a musical group called the Quarrymen. By 1962 the group included three other Liverpool lads: Paul McCartney, George Harrison, and Ringo Starr. Now they were called the Beatles.

During the 1960s, the Beatles performed all over the world. They were recognized and mobbed everywhere they went. By the end of the decade, they had become the most popular rock 'n' roll group of all time.

The Beatles broke up in 1970. John Lennon remained very popular, however. At the time of his death, Lennon was married to Japanese artist Yoko Ono. For years, the couple projected the image of gentle love that Lennon described in his songs. He and Yoko Ono were crusaders in the movement for world peace. All his life, John Lennon had stood for peace and understanding among all people. His shockingly violent death saddened and angered people everywhere.

Lennon's killer, Mark Chapman, was sentenced to 20 years to life in prison. His senseless act left a huge hole in the world of popular music. ■

The day after Lennon's murder, newspapers carried the tragic details.

During the 1960s, John Lennon (right) and his fellow Beatles became the most famous pop music group in history.

Reagan Era Begins
America Turns to the Right

Just two weeks after his brush with an assassin's bullet, President Reagan had recovered enough to return to the White House.

January 20, 1981, was a day for flag-waving and celebration. It was inauguration day for America's 40th president, Ronald Reagan. And, after 444 days in captivity, the U.S. hostages in Iran were freed.

During his campaign, Reagan had often criticized the role of "big government." Now his inaugural address was meant to reassure the public. "It's not my intention to do away with government," Reagan said. "It is rather to make it work—work with us, not over us; to stand by our side, not ride on our back."

Reagan believed that less government was better government. He was ready to launch the United States into a new era. During the Great Depression of the 1930s, President Franklin Roosevelt had offered America a "New Deal." He developed federal programs that put people to work. He put added responsibilities on the shoulders of the government. During the 1960s, Presidents Kennedy and Johnson supported strong federal programs, too.

Now Ronald Reagan was reversing this trend of federal responsibility. In his inaugural speech, he said, "Government is not the solution to our problem; government *is* the problem."

Social agencies protested. They pointed out that those who needed services the most would be hurt by government cutbacks. State and local governments wondered how they might finance programs that the federal government was going to cut. Still, many people seemed to agree with Reagan. The mood of the country had changed. Gone were the liberal, left-wing, pro-government-spending days of the sixties. In their place came the conservative, right-wing, anti-government-spending eighties.

Barely two months after Reagan took office, however, all these concerns were put aside. On March 30, 1981, six shots from the gun of a crazed assassin gave the nation another worry.

The Lovesick Assassin

The loud crack of gunfire shattered a sunny Monday after-noon in the nation's capital. It was 2:30 P.M., and Ronald Reagan had just stepped out of the Hilton Hotel in Washington. A crowd had gathered, and everyone wanted to get a glimpse of the new president.

As the shots rang out, those with the president tried to shield him. Bullets hit and seriously wounded a police officer, a Secret Service agent, and White House Press Secretary James Brady. Another Secret Service agent threw the president into the waiting car. The color drained from Reagan's face. He had been hit.

As the president's car raced away, Secret Service agents and police wrestled the gunman to the ground.

At George Washington University Hospital, doctors

removed the bullet from Reagan's left lung. The bullet had struck him very close to the heart. An inch or two closer, the wound could have been fatal.

"Does anybody know what that guy's beef was?" Reagan asked after hearing that the gunman had been captured. In truth, the would-be assassin was not interested in politics at all. John Hinckley, Jr., was a drifter, the son of a wealthy Texas oilman. After watching one of actress Jodie Foster's movies, he had fallen in love with her. An assassination scene in the movie had given Hinckley an insane idea. He decided he would show his love for Foster by killing the president. When he came to trial, Hinckley was declared insane and sent to a mental hospital.

The 70-year-old president made a remarkable recovery. He was soon back in the White House putting his campaign promises into action.

Tax Cuts, Budgets, Bombs

"In 1981, we cut your tax rates by nearly 25 percent," Reagan proudly told Americans in 1982. Reagan credited this tax cut for stopping inflation and lowering interest rates. In part, that was true. But an economic recession in 1981–1982 also brought interest rates down and halted rising inflation.

Critics said that Reagan's tax cuts favored the wealthy. Corporations that benefitted from the cuts did little to help the average American. Unemployment hit a high of 11 percent in 1982. The basic industries of steel, manufacturing, and coal mining were in decline. Automobile production reached an all-time low. With so many Americans out of work, it was no wonder that goods were not

selling and inflation was down. Lower interest rates meant little to the jobless who had no money to invest.

As he had promised, President Reagan cut government spending in many areas. However, he was still not able to balance the budget. In fact, the national debt grew. It reached $110 billion in 1982 and $195 billion in 1983. Reagan was cutting programs that aided the needy, protected the environment, and supported public education. But he was spending much more on defense.

In 1983, Reagan announced a plan called the Strategic Defense Initiative. It was quickly nicknamed "Star Wars." Star Wars was a satellite shield system that used laser beams to detect hostile missiles. It could shoot them down in mid-air before they could strike. Reagan asked Congress for $26 billion over five years to develop the program.

Critics were outraged. Some warned that it would never work. Even if 95 percent of the nuclear missiles were intercepted, they said, the remaining 5 percent would destroy the United States anyway. Some members of Congress worried that work on Star Wars would upset arms reduction talks with the Soviet Union. Others complained that such huge sums of money would be better spent on social programs. Reagan declared that the system was vital to America's defense. With his strong urging, the development of Star Wars began.

Watchdog of the World

Ever since his early days in politics, Reagan had been concerned with the threat of Soviet communism. His weapons build-up reflected that concern. So

Unemployment was high during the 1982 recession, and demonstrations such as this one took place in many cities.

did his foreign policy in Central America. When Reagan saw Communist aggression, he acted. He sent the government of El Salvador arms to fight Communist rebels. He supported the Contra rebels who were fighting the Communist Sandinista government of Nicaragua. In 1983, Reagan sent Marines to the Caribbean island of Grenada to halt a Communist takeover.

Reagan also sent U.S. troops to the Middle East. They arrived in Beirut, Lebanon, in August 1982 as part of an international peacekeeping force. The troops sought to control an ugly civil war between Christian and Muslim religious groups. In October 1983, a Muslim terrorist killed 237 Marines in Beirut. Critics wondered if America should really be policing the world. Many Americans recalled the Vietnam War. People were once again questioning the wisdom of involving U.S. troops in another nation's military struggles.

Patriotism and Popularity

Despite criticisms and controversy, Ronald Reagan was a popular president. He took his ideas directly to the American people in televised speeches. Many people liked his easygoing style. They nicknamed him "The Great Communicator." Meanwhile, his opponents recalled his background as an actor. They accused him of reading a script and of "playing a role." Even his critics, however, could not deny Reagan's popularity. He communicated a feeling of patriotism and national pride that many Americans felt had been missing for a long time.

As the 1984 election neared, employment was back up and inflation was down. Much of the country was enjoying an improving economy and a sense of national strength. President Reagan would be a tough candidate to challenge for reelection. ■

Sandra Day O'Connor: History-Making Judge

In 1981, Arizona Court of Appeals judge Sandra Day O'Connor made history. She donned the black robes of an associate justice of the U.S. Supreme Court. Her appointment on September 21 was one of Ronald Reagan's early acts as president. It was a popular choice. The Senate voted 99–0 to confirm the appointment. When O'Connor took the judicial oath, she became the first woman to sit on the highest court in the land.

Like Reagan, O'Connor was considered a conservative. Her record as a judge before her appointment was a major reason why Reagan chose her. In the past, she had often upheld states' rights in disputes with the federal government. She was also a strong supporter of law-enforcement rules. Both positions were popular with conservatives.

When O'Connor was appointed, many women hoped that she would use her seat on the court to champion women's rights. But throughout the decade, her judicial opinions showed no slant in that direction. Rather, she remained true to the conservative views that had brought her to the court in the first place. ■

Sandra Day O'Connor, the first woman justice ever appointed to the United States Supreme Court.

The Civil War Over Abortion

Men and women marched like grim warriors outside the medical clinic. They carried signs that read "Abortion, No! Life, Yes!"

An equally determined group gathered across the street. "Freedom of choice!" they shouted. "Protect our rights!"

The debate on abortion rights divided Americans more than any other social issue during the 1980s. A Texas court case called *Roe v. Wade* brought the issue before the Supreme Court in 1973. The court then ruled that a state may not prevent a woman from having an abortion during her first six months of pregnancy.

Many Americans applauded the ruling. They favored a woman's right to make a choice. It was wrong, they maintained, to force a woman to continue an unwanted pregnancy. They called the *Roe v. Wade* decision a step forward.

Anti-abortion forces protested the decision. They argued that a fetus is a human being and must be protected from murder. The unborn child at any stage, they declared, has a right to life.

The sides were clearly drawn, and there were few who stood in the middle. Pro-life advocates, or "Right-to-Lifers," carried signs outside clinics that performed abortions. Sometimes they blocked entrances and made it difficult for patients to enter. They begged women to consider adoption rather than abortion.

The other side described themselves as pro-choice. They supported abortion rights. They believed in a woman's right to decide what happens to her own body. "Keep your laws off my body!" said their banners. Many

During the decade, opponents and supporters of abortion often confronted each other in demonstrations around the country.

of the pro-choice supporters were women. They were angry that women's rights were being decided by a largely male government.

Supreme Court Limits Right to Abortion

Several states tried to limit the rights granted by *Roe v. Wade*. Some states passed laws requiring a woman's husband to give his consent before she could get an abortion. Other states said that the parents of a minor must be notified before an abortion could be performed. Some states barred the use of state facilities for abortions. In a series of rulings throughout the 1980s, the Supreme Court

upheld many of these tougher state laws.

Each of these rulings limited a woman's right to abortion. As expected, each brought mixed reactions. Pro-choice supporters called each decision "a sad day for freedom." They worried that the court was moving toward completely overturning *Roe v. Wade*. Pro-lifers considered each limit a victory.

By the end of the decade, a more conservative Supreme Court seemed likely to further restrict abortion rights. Pro-choice supporters worried about the future of their cause. Right-to-lifers were encouraged. And the political tug-of-war over abortion rights continued into the 1990s. ■

In 1984, Democratic presidential nominee Walter Mondale chose Geraldine Ferraro as his vice-presidential running mate. It was the first time a woman had been chosen for that spot.

Reagan Reelected in Landslide Victory

"**H**e's unbeatable!" said many Americans. They were talking about their 40th president, Ronald Reagan. It was 1984, and Reagan and his vice president, George Bush, were seeking election to a second term of office. America was enjoying rising prosperity and a sense of national pride. Republicans made it clear that the Reagan–Bush ticket stood for traditional values of patriotism, religious faith, and high family ideals.

The Democrats searched hard to find a candidate to challenge the popular president. They chose former vice president Walter Mondale. Mondale made political history by choosing New York congresswoman Geraldine Ferraro as his vice-presidential running mate. No major American political party had ever before chosen a

woman for its national ticket.

During the campaign, Mondale attacked the president's runaway budget. He criticized Reagan's policy of increasing defense spending while at the same time cutting programs that helped the needy and protected the environment. He said the way to control the budget was not by slashing spending, but by raising taxes.

Higher taxes are seldom popular. When the candidates met for two televised debates, Reagan criticized Mondale's tax increase plan.

Actually, the president made a poor showing during the first debate. The 73-year-old Reagan appeared tired and confused. "Is Oldest U.S. President Showing His Age?" asked newspaper headlines the next day. In the next debate, however, Reagan

seemed better prepared and more vigorous.

Early surveys showed the president ahead. When the votes came in, though, Reagan's margin of victory was even greater than expected. He captured every state except Mondale's home state, Minnesota, as well as the District of Columbia. Some of the president's support was a surprise. Of voters between 18 and 24, some 59 percent cast their ballots for America's oldest president.

Reagan predicted that history would recall his second term as the golden years . . .

Inauguration day 1985 fell on a Sunday, so Reagan took his oath of office in a private ceremony. The next day he gave a public address. Freezing weather gripped Washington D.C. For the first time since 1833, the president did not hold an inauguration parade down Pennsylvania Avenue. Spirits were high despite the cold. Reagan predicted that history would recall his second term as "the golden years—when the American Revolution was reborn, when freedom gained new life and America reached for the best. . . ." ∎

A Political Roller Coaster

Reagan's Second Term: A Series of Highs and Lows

The president's second term began with some life-and-death decisions. International terrorists were threatening American lives. In June 1985, Muslim militants hijacked a TWA jet with many Americans on board. Reagan had to make a hard choice. Should the United States attack and try to capture the hijackers, or should it hold back? In this case, Reagan showed restraint.

"I could get mad enough now to think of a couple of things we could do to retaliate," the president said. "But I would probably be sentencing a number of Americans to death if I did it. I have to wait it out as long as those people are there, threatened and alive." The president's patience paid off. All but one of the hostages were eventually released unharmed.

Reagan's patience wore thin, however, when it came to Libyan dictator Colonel Muammar al-Qadhafi. Qadhafi openly provided Arab terrorists with arms and support. Reagan warned Qadhafi that acts of terrorism would not be tolerated. Qadhafi ignored the warning. In April 1986, Libya was blamed for a bomb that exploded in a Berlin nightclub. The club, a popular stop for U.S. servicemembers, was destroyed. One American soldier died in the blast.

This time Reagan decided restraint was not the answer. On April 15, the United States struck back. In a half-hour surprise attack, 2,000 American bombs rained down on terrorist bases in Libya. The attack stunned Libya and the rest of the world.

"We have done what we had to do," declared President Reagan. "If necessary, we shall do it again." Many nations criticized the bloodshed in Libya. Others praised the president's strong stand against terrorism.

A High Point: Beginning of End of Cold War

During Reagan's second term, America's chilly relations with the Soviet Union began to thaw. In 1985, Mikhail Gorbachev became the new Soviet leader. Gorbachev brought new vision and new ideas to the Soviet government. He was anxious to talk of peace.

Reagan and Gorbachev met to discuss ways to reduce the threat of nuclear war. They found they could get along. Reagan had once called the Soviet Union the "Evil Empire." But now newspapers showed Reagan and Gorbachev smiling and shaking hands. "There is good chemistry between us," Reagan said.

The U.S.–Soviet meetings eventually led to the signing of a historic weapons treaty in 1987. Both America and the Soviet Union agreed to destroy hundreds of nuclear missiles.

After the Iran–Contra scandal became public, President Reagan appointed his own review board to investigate the matter. Here the president meets with the panel's three members, from left to right, former senator John Tower, former senator Edmund Muskie, and former National Security Adviser Brent Scowcroft.

41

A Low Point: Iran–Contra Scandal

Was it a coverup, or a bad mistake? Americans wanted answers about a secret arms deal with the Middle Eastern country of Iran. U.S. policy forbade trading arms for political hostages. Yet it was discovered that the Reagan administration secretly sold missiles and missile parts to Iran. After the weapons were delivered, Iranians persuaded terrorists in Lebanon to release some U.S. hostages.

News of this secret arms deal became public in November 1986. And there was more to the scandal. Profits from the arms sales had been illegally used to aid the Contras, an army of Nicaraguan rebels. Reagan had strongly supported the Contras' fight to overthrow Nicaragua's Communist Sandinista government. But the U.S. Congress, unwilling to back a foreign civil war, had cut off Contra aid in 1983.

Marine Lieutenant Colonel Oliver North was charged with running the Contra aid operation. North was a staff member of the U.S. National Security Council (NSC). In a televised congressional hearing in July 1987, North admitted secretly funneling money to the Contras. He insisted, however, that he had been following orders from superiors. "I assumed the president was aware of what I was doing and approved," he said. Some Americans believed North. They believed that he was a patriotic hero who had been used as a scapegoat by the officials above him. Others called Oliver North a liar and a criminal.

Higher officials were hit by the fallout of the Iran–Contra scandal. NSC chief Vice Admiral John Poindexter and White House Chief of Staff Donald Regan were forced to resign.

What about the president? Americans wanted to know. Did Reagan authorize the secret dealings? Was he aware of the activities? Reagan denied any knowledge of the affair. He did admit, however, that the scandal was a stain on his record.

In the end, the American people seemed to believe the president. However, the scandal badly damaged Reagan's popularity in his second term.

Reagan's Farewell

As Reagan's presidency neared its end, unemployment was down and inflation was in check. But the national debt had grown ever larger. The United States owed billions of dollars to foreign investors. And Americans cast a wary eye at a government that pulled off secret dealings with or without the president's knowledge. Despite these troubles, Reagan's vice president, Republican George Bush, won the White House in 1988. (See story on page 47.)

On January 11, 1989, Ronald Reagan said farewell to the American people. Following a 200-year-old custom, the president delivered a final address to the nation. He reported on the state of America. He applauded the nation's "restored sense of patriotism." He praised his two terms in office as a time that had made America "stronger and freer."

Most Americans, whether they supported Reagan or not, took note of one encouraging fact. For the first time in nearly 30 years, after assassinations, scandals, and failed presidencies, a presidential term had come to a peaceful and successful conclusion. ∎

Marine Lieutenant Colonel Oliver North testified before Congress about his role in the Iran–Contra scandal.

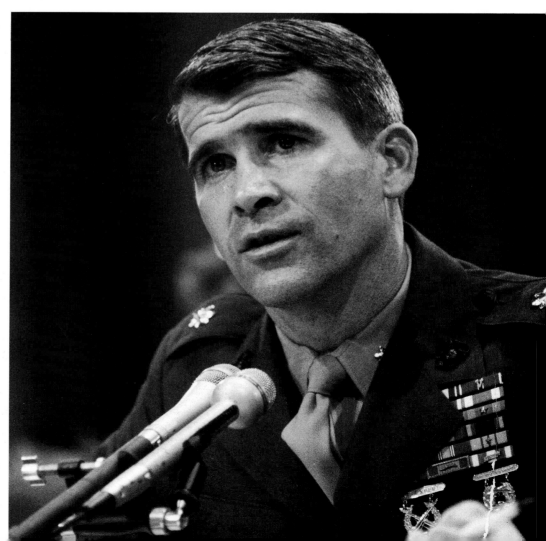

By the late 1980s, the Supreme Court had become more conservative due to President Reagan's appointments.

Reagan Conservatives Control Supreme Court

During his two terms in office, Ronald Reagan had filled several seats on the U.S. Supreme Court with right-wing conservatives. His first appointment in 1981 made Sandra Day O'Connor the first woman ever to hold a seat on the court.

In 1986, Reagan named William H. Rehnquist, an associate justice since 1972, to replace retiring Chief Justice Warren Burger. Many liberals opposed Rehnquist's appointment as head of the court. They said his conservative record showed too little concern for minority groups and civil liberties.

Antonin Scalia filled the associate justice position left by Rehnquist. Scalia was the first person of Italian descent to serve on the Supreme Court. Scalia's conservative views and his decisions as a federal appeals court judge earned him his appointment.

Reagan had to try, try, and try again to fill the next court opening. When 79-year-old Justice Lewis F. Powell, Jr., announced his retirement in 1987, Reagan nominated the very conservative Judge Robert H. Bork to replace him. Bork's appointment, however, met with strong opposition from the Democratic-controlled Senate.

Many senators charged that Bork's strong opinions on civil rights and civil liberties issues put him too far to the right. Representatives from women's groups and civil rights groups also spoke against the nomination. Bork testified that he had changed his views somewhat in recent years. Still, the Senate voted 58–42 against Bork's confirmation.

Reagan's second candidate for the spot was another conservative, Judge Douglas H. Ginsburg. But a few days after his nomination, it was reported that Ginsburg had smoked marijuana while in law school. He withdrew his name from consideration.

In a third try, President Reagan nominated Judge Anthony M. Kennedy of Sacramento, California. Kennedy was thought to be a more moderate conservative. This time the Senate easily confirmed the nomination.

By 1989, four of the nine members of the Supreme Court were Reagan appointees. The president's conservative views were well represented on the court. Liberals worried about how the justices would rule on abortion rights, civil rights, and separation of church and state. Presidents come and go after eight years since they're limited to only two terms of office. But Supreme Court justices hold lifetime appointments. The shift to the right would be reflected in Supreme Court decisions for a long time to come. ■

Tragedy in Space

Space Shuttle *Challenger* Explodes After Liftoff

The morning of January 28, 1986, dawned clear and unusually cold in Cape Canaveral, Florida. However, all plans for launching America's 25th space-shuttle flight were proceeding normally. After a moderate delay to clear ice from the launching pad, the countdown to launch *Challenger* resumed at 11:38 A.M.

Ten seconds later *Challenger* thrust upward, engines blazing. Its rockets trailed white smoke. On the ground, thousands of spectators gasped in wonder. Friends and relatives of the seven crewmembers filled rows of bleachers. They waved banners and cheered. Millions of Americans watching on television took pride at another successful advance by the U.S. space program.

Challenger soared to a height of nine miles. The shuttle commander, Dick Scobee, sig-naled a power increase. "Roger, go with throttle up, up," ground control heard him say.

Suddenly, 73 seconds after liftoff, *Challenger* burst into an orange-white ball of fire. The spacecraft exploded into thousands of pieces that rained into the Atlantic Ocean. Many of the onlookers on the ground were speechless with shock. Others screamed in disbelief. It was soon clear that no one aboard could have survived the explosion.

The disaster was the worst in America's 25 years of manned space exploration. The tragedy was especially hard-felt because the first private citizen to journey into space was on board.

High School Teacher Joins Space Program

In 1984, President Reagan had announced a space flight participant program. The National Aeronautics and Space Administration (NASA) would select an American teacher to join a shuttle crew. More than 11,000 educators applied for the position. A New Hampshire teacher, 36-year-old Christa McAuliffe, was finally selected.

The crew of the ill-fated Space Shuttle *Challenger:* Back row, from left to right: Ellison Onizuka, Christa McAuliffe, Greg Jarvis, and Judy Resnik. Front row, left to right: Mike Smith, Dick Scobee, and Ronald McNair.

McAuliffe's students, her husband, and her two children shared in the excitement.

As a "citizen observer," it was McAuliffe's job to build enthusiasm and interest in the U.S. space program. At the Johnson Space Center, she made friends with her fellow crewmembers. Most of them were space-travel veterans. Commander Dick Scobee had been on a 1984 *Challenger* voyage. Judith Resnik, Michael Smith, Ellison Onizuka, and Ronald McNair had also flown shuttle missions before. Only crewmember Gregory Jarvis would be, like Christa McAuliffe, a first-time space traveler.

Americans were stunned by the tragedy they saw on their television screens that day.

McAuliffe's students and friends had packed the Concord High School auditorium in New Hampshire to watch the *Challenger* launch on television. At liftoff, they burst into cheers. But seconds later their cheering turned to sobs and screams.

What Went Wrong?

Americans were stunned by the tragedy they saw on their television screens that day. The *Challenger* disaster stunned NASA as well. All the earlier space-shuttle flights had been extremely successful. They all performed well, launching communications satellites and conducting experiments in space. Now, after numerous flawless flights and intense safety programs, a $4 billion spacecraft had blown into bits and killed its crew.

Engineers carefully inspected recovered pieces of the shuttle. They reviewed films of the fateful launch and listened to tapes from the cockpit voice recorder. The tapes revealed that the crew on board knew only briefly that there were problems. The first and last recorded hint of trouble came just before the explosion. It was the voice of pilot Mike Smith. "Uh, oh," he had said.

The investigation found that a fuel leak from a faulty seal had caused *Challenger* to explode. Investigators said that earlier ground tests and failures should have alerted NASA to the possibility of problems. A final review revealed that some engineers had suggested the launch be delayed. In late 1986, a congressional report came out. It said there were too many pressures on NASA to fly shuttles more and more often. This pressure, the report concluded, set the stage for disaster.

The loss of the *Challenger* closed down the U.S. manned space program. While shuttle engineers worked on new safety measures, the government evaluated the goals of the whole space program.

America Returns to Space

NASA spent 32 months in serious research and redesign. On September 29, 1988, the shuttle *Discovery* stood ready to blast into orbit with five crewmembers aboard. The tension mounted as *Discovery* rose from the pad. It seemed like an eternity until the shuttle passed the 73-second mark, the point at which *Challenger* had exploded. A huge sigh of relief came from NASA ground control as Space Shuttle *Discovery* made it safely into space.

Six hours later, the shuttle crew launched a new communications satellite. The rest of the mission went smoothly. Declared one NASA official, "We're back in business!" ■

Back on track and flying high: The launch of the Space Shuttle *Discovery* marked America's successful return to space after the *Challenger* tragedy.

America Declares War on Drugs

A New Jersey narcotics officer views some of the heroin, cocaine, marijuana, and large amounts of cash that were seized in a major drug raid. More than a dozen people were arrested.

Whole sections of cities had become wastelands ruled by street gangs. Violent crimes were on the rise, and most were related to a single root cause. People died needlessly, and families were torn apart. America during the 1980s was a nation plagued by drug and alcohol abuse. It was time for action. The U.S. government named drug abuse the enemy and declared war on it.

Drug users were turning to new, powerful drugs. "Crack," an addictive, smokable form of cocaine, was cheap. It was also dangerous. An overdose could kill almost instantly. Heroin now posed an even greater threat. Addicts ran the added risk of getting AIDS from infected needles. The government put out a warning. A single dose of cocaine, it stated, could kill. Still, while the use of other illegal drugs was going down, cocaine use was on the rise. Deaths caused by cocaine use tripled between 1981 and 1986.

Stopping the Flow

President Reagan increased spending on drug education, treatment programs, and law enforcement. He called for stiffer penalties for drug trafficking. Nancy Reagan, the president's wife, made the war on drugs her special cause. She traveled widely and appeared on television and radio. "Say 'yes'

to life," she urged young people. "And when it comes to drugs and alcohol, just say 'no.' "

The Reagan administration said it was determined to stop the flow of drugs from Latin America. In 1986, the president sent U.S. troops to aid Bolivia in its war against drug traffickers. U.S. and Bolivian forces together raided cocaine labs hidden in the jungles.

In 1989, the United States authorized $65 million in aid to support Colombia's war on the drug trade. Other Latin American governments such as Mexico worked harder to curb drug trafficking as well.

"Drug Czar" Bennett Helps Bush Wage War

In 1988, Congress created a new post—the director of national drug control policy. In 1989, President Bush appointed former Secretary of Education William J. Bennett to the position. It was his job to lead the effort to reduce drug usage in

the country. He became known as the "Drug Czar."

Bennett's program was strong on law enforcement. He supported stiff penalties for drug criminals. These penalties included "boot camps" that put convicts through tough physical training. Critics said Bennett's boot camp plan would only result in "a healthier collection of drug dealers and addicts."

At a September 1990 press conference, Bush and Bennett declared that America was winning the war. Bennett said the use of cocaine was down and that Latin American drug lords were on the run. Many others, however, said Bennett's programs were not providing enough money for drug treatment and education programs. Statistics also showed that drug-related crime was still a major problem on the streets of many American cities.

The government may have declared a war on drugs during the 1980s, but that war was a long way from being won. ∎

George Bush Defeats Michael Dukakis in 1988 Election

George Bush had served for eight years as Ronald Reagan's vice president. Now he wanted to take the helm himself. Bush had been thought of as a quiet, mild-mannered man. In 1988, though, he ran a very tough campaign. In fact, that year's presidential campaign became known as the most negative in the nation's history.

Republicans had nominated George Bush as their presidential candidate at their convention in August. The 64-year-old World War II hero had made a bid for the Republican nomination once before. In 1980 he lost out to Ronald Reagan. Reagan later surprised many by naming Bush as his vice-presidential running mate.

Bush proudly accepted the 1988 nomination, pledging to "keep America moving forward, always forward." He selected Indiana senator J. Danforth Quayle as his running mate. Republicans thought the young, good-looking Quayle would have great voter appeal.

The Democrats chose Massachusetts governor Michael Dukakis to run against Bush. Dukakis called for honest government and national change. He selected Texas senator Lloyd Bentsen as his vice-presidential running mate.

During the campaign, Bush said what many people wanted to hear. He spoke of America's greatness and described the nation's many voluntary organi-

zations as "spread like stars, like a thousand points of light in a broad and peaceful sky." While Michael Dukakis suggested raising taxes to balance the budget, Bush promised Americans that he would let them keep their money. "Read my lips," he exclaimed. "No new taxes!"

Mud-Slinging Campaign

The campaign heated up as both Republicans and Democrats turned to smear tactics. Bush attacked Governor Dukakis for his record in Massachusetts. He blamed Dukakis for pollution in Boston Harbor. He accused the governor of allowing vicious prisoners to be released on furloughs from prison. The Republicans labeled Dukakis as too liberal and out of touch with the American mainstream.

Dukakis fought back, saying that Bush was "dragging the truth into the gutter." Dukakis supporters pointed to the problems of the Reagan era. They noted the runaway budget and recalled the Iran–Contra scandal Democrats asked if Bush had anything to hide.

Democrats found plenty to criticize about vice-presidential candidate Dan Quayle. They quickly uncovered Quayle's weak performance in college. They also pointed out that he had spent the Vietnam War years in the Indiana National Guard. They charged that Quayle used

Democrat Michael Dukakis challenged Republican George Bush for the presidency in 1988. Dukakis lost.

family influence to get a desk job while other young Americans were in combat. Critics pointed out the pro-military positions Quayle took as senator. They suggested he was willing to send others to war, but was not willing to fight himself.

Bush Elected President; Democrats Win Congress

In November, George Bush was elected president with nearly 54 percent of the vote. He won the electoral vote by a count of 426 to 112. George

In 1989, George Bush took the oath of office as the nation's 41st president as his wife, Barbara, looked on.

Bush was the first sitting vice president since Martin Van Buren in 1836 to be elected president in his own right.

While Republicans kept the White House, the Democrats held control of the Senate and the House of Representatives. The term ahead was bound to bring some political struggles between the president and Congress.

Bush's First Year Brings Little Change

Bush had been Reagan's loyal vice president. Now, in his first year in office, President Bush remained true to Reagan's policies. He kept a conservative reign on Congress, vetoing pro-choice legislation. He also vetoed a bill that would have raised the minimum wage. Supporters of the wage-hike bill said the increase would help the poor. Bush, like Reagan, was concerned with inflation. He

insisted that higher wages would inflate prices.

Bush continued Reagan's efforts to better U.S.–Soviet relations. He held summit meetings with Soviet leader Gorbachev. At first Bush appeared cautious about Gorbachev's sincerity. But once he was convinced that Gorbachev truly sought reform, Bush offered economic aid to the Soviets.

President Bush continued efforts to keep domestic spending down. Rather than increase government aid, he encouraged volunteer programs to help the homeless, AIDS victims, and the illiterate. He proposed establishing a foundation called the Points of Light Initiative. The group would assist private efforts to help the needy.

In his inaugural address, George Bush had promised that "a new breeze was blowing" in America. During his first year in office, however, the breeze seemed to blow directly out of the Reagan years. ∎

The Forces of Nature Let Loose with a Fury

Twice during the 1980s, Mother Nature let loose with demonstrations of the forces that shape this planet. These two natural disasters framed the decade like two very spectacular bookends.

Mount Saint Helens Blast Stuns Northwest

A massive explosion, about 500 times more powerful than an atomic bomb, blew away the top of Mount Saint Helens in Washington on May 18, 1980. The eruption of the volcano showered mud, rock, and ash over the immediate area, killing at least 70 people. Hot mud clogged rivers, destroying millions of salmon and trout. Elk, birds, deer, farm animals, and pets were caught in the mud flow or killed by the intense heat. A hundred thousand acres of forest became a dead zone.

When Mount Saint Helens blew its top, the boom was heard 135 miles away. Skies became black as night as ash drifted on the winds over parts of Washington, Oregon, and Idaho. Ash clogged machinery and ruined engines. Residents of the Northwest worried about breathing the gritty air. Many wore surgical masks to protect their lungs. The beauty of spring and early summer was shrouded in volcanic ash.

By summer's end, the ash settled and a lava dome plugged the hole in Mount Saint Helens. Then tourists began returning to see the Martian-like landscape. They came away with souvenir packages of ash and a great deal of respect for Mother Nature.

San Francisco Bay Area Hit by Major Quake

A massive earthquake hit the San Francisco Bay Area on the evening of October 17, 1989. The quake measured 7.1 on the Richter scale. It was centered

A 50-foot section of the San Francisco–Oakland Bay Bridge collapsed during the 1989 earthquake.

just northeast of Santa Cruz, some 75 miles south of San Francisco, along the San Andreas fault.

The 15 seconds of rumbling brought huge blocks of concrete from an Oakland highway crashing down on cars below. A 50-foot upper section of the San Francisco–Oakland Bay Bridge collapsed. Buildings in San Francisco's Marina District buckled, and fires raged from broken gas lines. In the seaside town of Santa Cruz, downtown buildings collapsed into heaps of rubble. When the smoke and dust had cleared, at least 60 people had lost their lives.

The third game of baseball's World Series between the Oakland A's and the San Francisco Giants was about to begin when the quake hit. The huge crowd at Candlestick Park fell silent as the earth began to shake. Seats rocked and light posts swayed. Fortunately, damage at Candlestick was minor. However, it was a solemn, anxious crowd that left the ball park after the game was called off. Like everyone in the area, these people worried about the safety of their friends and loved ones.

Death and destruction could have been more widespread, but Californians helped one another. Residents searched their neighborhoods for injured victims. Volunteers quickly helped set up shelters for the homeless. Earthquake preparations paid off as trained disaster specialists calmly went to work. However, it took many months before things returned to normal for Bay Area residents. ■

Medical Advances Bring Stunning Changes in Heart Transplants

Barney Clark's heart was failing. Soon he would die. So on December 2, 1982, a surgical team at the University of Utah Medical Center took a first-time drastic step. They cut away the lower half of Clark's diseased heart. They replaced it with a mechanical heart made of plastic and aluminum. Barney Clark, a 61-year-old retired dentist from Seattle, Washington, thus became the first person in the world to receive a permanent artificial heart.

The mechanical heart is called the Jarvik-7, after its inventor, Robert Jarvik. The heart is powered by an air compressor. The power source remains outside the patient's body. It is connected to the heart by a pair of plastic hoses.

An artificial heart was first used in 1969. The mechanical heart kept blood circulating inside the patient's chest for 60 hours until a suitable human heart became available for transplant.

Barney Clark received the first artificial heart intended as a permanent replacement for a human heart. He died 112 days after the surgery, when his own internal organs failed.

A second artificial-heart implant was performed in Louisville, Kentucky, in 1984. The patient, 54-year-old William J. Schroeder, suffered a series of strokes shortly after surgery. He recovered enough to leave the hospital, though. Schroeder survived 620 days, becoming the longest-living person to receive the Jarvik-7.

Because of the danger of stroke, many doctors have questioned the use of the artificial heart as a permanent implant. Some argued that the Jarvik-7 should only be used for patients awaiting a human heart transplant. In 1990, the U.S. Food and Drug Administration (FDA) withdrew its approval for the use of the Jarvik heart.

Human heart transplants became quite common and successful during the 1980s. New drugs became available that fought infection and reduced organ rejection. But finding and transporting donor organs continued to be a problem.

When acceptable donor hearts were not available, doctors sometimes turned to extraordinary measures. In 1984, surgeons at Loma Linda University Medical Center in California transplanted a baboon's heart into a 15-day-old infant born with a fatal heart defect. The baby died 21 days after the transplant. The operation stirred controversy. Some doctors questioned performing such a highly experimental operation on a human being.

Advances in technology during the 1980s offered second chances at life to many patients. But they also brought the medical community face to face with some new—and difficult—questions to answer. ∎

William Schroeder was able to undergo a full workout on a stationary bicycle after his heart transplant.

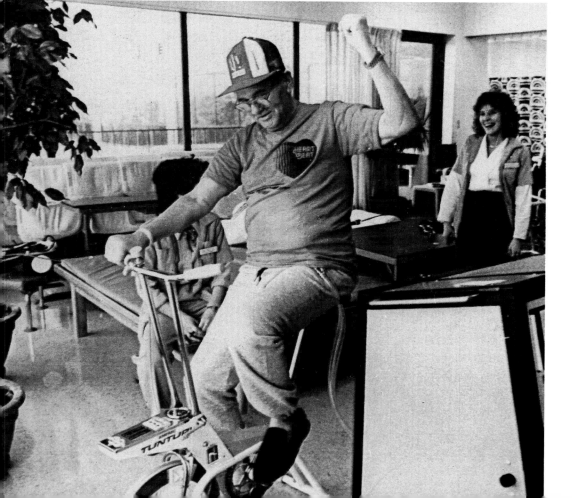

Terrible Price of Progress

Disaster at Chernobyl Nuclear Power Plant

An explosion ripped apart a nuclear reactor in the Soviet Union on April 26, 1986. The explosion occurred at the Chernobyl power plant, located about 70 miles north of the city of Kiev. The force of the blast blew the roof off the plant building and launched radioactive material into the air. It was the world's worst nuclear accident.

The Soviet Union did not immediately release news of the disaster. But on April 28, radiation detection devices in Sweden picked up unusually high readings. It became clear that air blowing into Sweden from the Soviet Union was carrying radioactive particles. Only then did the Soviets issue an announcement that an "accident" had occurred at Chernobyl.

Soon the fallout from Chernobyl rained down on many parts of Europe. Radiation counts skyrocketed to 100,000 times the normal amounts. The fallout contaminated farm crops and grazing lands in Sweden, Norway, Finland, Poland, Scotland, and Great Britain.

Soviet doctors rushed to the Chernobyl site to examine workers and residents. Nearly 300 severely injured victims were sent to Moscow hospitals. By year's end, the nuclear accident had claimed the lives of at least 31 Soviet citizens, mostly plant workers and firefighters.

A Soviet report concluded that human error had caused the Chernobyl accident. When workers lost control of the reactor, a huge power surge set

Children in Warsaw, Poland, were given an iodine solution to help protect them from nuclear fallout from Chernobyl.

off the explosion. The report admitted that other Soviet plants, like the Chernobyl station, had no way to contain radioactive materials during an accident. U.S. nuclear plants do have such safeguards.

The Chernobyl disaster brought to the forefront one of the hottest issues of the decade: Were the rewards of nuclear

power worth the possible deadly risks? Scientists and engineers around the world worked hard to develop better safeguards for nuclear power plants. Meanwhile, concerned protesters worked just as hard to shut the plants down. Both sides could agree on one thing. The world could not afford another Chernobyl. ∎

The Eighties Olympics
Miracles, Boycotts, and . . .

"**D**o you believe in *miracles*!?" The sportscaster shouted into his microphone, as the final seconds ticked away and the crowd roared. Then he answered his own question: YES! The scene was Lake Placid, New York. The time was February 1980. And the event was the Olympic hockey match between the United States and the Soviet Union.

The U.S. team's 4–3 victory in that game was, in the opinion of many, indeed a miracle. A squad of 20 U.S. college students defeated what experts said was the greatest hockey team in the world. When the American team went on to defeat Finland for the gold medal, that became *the* story of the 1980 Winter Olympics.

To be sure, there were other memorable performances at the 1980 games. Ingemar Stenmark of Sweden won gold medals in the men's slalom and giant slalom alpine skiing events, and Hanni Wenzel of tiny Liechtenstein did likewise in those two women's events. However, the standout single athlete was Eric Heiden, a 21-year-old from Wisconsin. Heiden swept every title in men's speed skating. He became the first athlete to win five gold medals in any Winter Olympics.

Americans Boycott 1980 Summer Olympics

Not a single American athlete won a medal at the 1980 Summer Olympics. In fact, not a single American athlete even showed up. The United States had called a boycott of the 22nd Summer Olympics held in Moscow in the Soviet Union.

The boycott was a political protest. In December 1979, the Soviet Union had invaded the country of Afghanistan. U.S. president Jimmy Carter demanded that Soviet troops withdraw. The Soviets refused. A few months before the games were to be held, Carter announced that the United States would not send its athletes or its money to a Communist aggressor.

President Carter's pressure on the U.S. Olympic Committee caused the committee to vote to keep the Americans at home. The decision moved some athletes to tears. Many had trained for years for their one shot at being in the Olympics.

More than 40 other nations followed America's lead, among them West Germany, China, Japan, and Canada. As was expected, the games were dominated by the Soviet Union

Members of the U.S. hockey team celebrate after scoring a goal against the Soviet team in the 1980 Olympics.

Medals

and its Communist allies, particularly East Germany. Between them the Soviets and East Germans won 14 gold medals in the men's track-and-field events, and another 11 in the women's. They were equally dominant in swimming, winning 9 gold medals in the men's events and 14 in the women's.

Soviets Call Revenge Boycott in '84

In 1984, the big Olympic news was another boycott—this time by the Soviet Union. The Soviets refused to send athletes to the summer games in Los Angeles, California. They said that private sponsorship of Olympic facilities made the Los Angeles games too commercial.

The Soviets also complained that security plans were weak and would not protect their athletes. The Soviet-bloc nations of East Germany, Czechoslovakia, Poland, Hungary, Bulgaria, and Cuba joined the boycott. Many Olympic organizers believed the Soviets were just striking back at the United States for its 1980 boycott of the Moscow Olympics.

America's Carl Lewis and Mary Lou Retton were the two stars of the Los Angeles Olympics. Lewis's talents in track and field brought him four gold medals. The 16-year-old Retton won five medals, including the gold in women's all-around gymnastics.

The United States won by far the most medals. But as in 1980, the competition suffered from the absence of some of the world's best athletes.

Seoul Games in 1988 Were Boycott-Free

Politics played almost no role in the 1988 Summer Olympics in Seoul, South Korea. There was, however, another problem that cast a dark cloud over the games: illegal drugs.

Canada's Ben Johnson had been called "the fastest man in the world," and the name seemed to fit. In Seoul, Johnson finished the 100-meter dash in record time. He outran his top rival, American Carl Lewis.

But just six days after his victory, Johnson left the games in disgrace. He had been stripped of his gold medal for using anabolic steroids. These dangerous drugs artificially increase physical stamina and improve performance. After Johnson was disqualified, the gold medal went to Lewis, the second place finisher. Johnson was not the only athlete to fail a drug test in Seoul. In all, ten athletes were disqualified for using illegal drugs.

U.S. track star Florence Griffith-Joyner caught the crowd's attention in Seoul. With her record-breaking speed and flashy style, "Flo-Jo" won three gold medals and one silver. Her sister-in-law, Jackie Joyner-Kersee, won the grueling heptathlon and the long jump.

The Soviet Union took home the most medals in Seoul, winning a total of 132, including 55 gold. The Soviets even beat the Americans at basketball. It was only the second time in Olympic history that an American basketball team failed to win the gold medal. ■

U.S. track star Florence Griffith-Joyner raises her arms in joy following her victory in the women's 100-meter dash at the 1988 Olympics.

The Big Bu$ine$$ of $port$

In 1979, Nolan Ryan became baseball's first—and only— million-dollar-a-year player. He signed baseball's richest contract, for $1.3 million, to pitch for the Houston Astros. Ten years and several million-dollar-a-year players later, Minnesota's Kirby Puckett signed baseball's new richest contract. This time it was for *$3 million* a year.

National Football League players went on strike twice during the 1980s.

The one thing that became clear during the 1980s was that sports had become more and more of a business—a big business. And like all businesses, sometimes the employees did not get along well with the management. The result was something that's bad for all businesses—labor strikes.

The 1981 baseball season brought the first sports strike of the decade. The strike resulted from a disagreement between the club owners and the players over the signing of free agents. The players didn't like the owner's plan that involved how a team would make up for the loss of a free agent. In June the players went on strike.

A compromise came after seven weeks, and players returned to the diamonds. The strike caused the cancellation of a total of 713 games. Fans were furious at both sides. The strike cost the players about $28 million in salaries. The clubs lost almost $116 million in sales.

Football Players Also Walk Out

Labor problems hit professional sports again in 1982. This time the National Football League players walked off the job. The players went on strike after the second game of the season. They complained that their salaries were low in comparison to other top professionals.

NFL owners had just signed a 5-year, $2 billion package with television networks to televise their games. The NFL Players Association asked for a share of the huge profits. When owners said no, the players struck.

With the season on hold, the players set up their own all-star league and scheduled 20 games. But only two games were played, and few fans showed up.

The strike lasted 57 days. In the end, management in-creased salary minimums, play-off money, and medical benefits. But public interest in the 1982 season had faded. There were plenty of empty seats for the remaining games of the season.

In 1987, NFL players once more took to the picket lines.

Things remained quiet on the sports labor-management front for the next several years. But in 1987, NFL players once again took to the picket lines. This time the players wanted free agency.

The walkout lasted 24 days. The players went back to work without having won any of their demands. The strike caused even more hard feelings between management and the players.

To many sports fans, none of these labor disputes made much sense. They believed that professional athletes have it made. These athletes get to spend many of their adult years playing games, while most other adults have to work for a living. In addition, the players get paid millions of dollars a year to do so. Fans couldn't understand why players would go on strike.

The players were aware, however, that during the 1980s sports had become a billion-dollar industry. All they wanted, they said, was their fair share of a very rich pie. ∎

Magic and Bird Soar to Great Heights

As the 1980s began, pro basketball's Los Angeles Lakers and Boston Celtics had just come off several less-than-successful seasons. Neither team had won a championship in years. All that was about to change, though—just like *magic*!

Beginning with the 1979–1980 season, the Lakers and Celtics each added one of the top two collegiate players in the country: The Lakers got Earvin "Magic" Johnson, and the Celtics got Larry Bird. The two had faced each other in the 1979 NCAA championship game. Johnson's Michigan State team had beaten Bird's Indiana State team, 75–64, for the title. No one knew it at the time, but it was to be the first of many memorable meetings between the two great players.

The Celtics and the Lakers made perfect rivals. The Celtics came from the East Coast. An old-fashioned team, they were noted for their gritty style, great teamwork, and skillful players. The Celtics reflected the city of Boston . . . traditional, serious, classic.

The Lakers came from the West Coast, from glitzy, glamorous L.A. Their byword was "showtime," and they had a razzle-dazzle style that fit their city. The Lakers played fast and hard, and they had famous movie stars in the crowd every night at their home games.

Magic Johnson was a 6'9" point guard who made the Laker offense go. By his second season, he had clearly become the team leader. His enthusiasm and on-the-court presence practically made him a second coach of the team. Johnson was also credited with pumping new life into the game of Lakers veteran superstar Kareem Abdul-Jabbar.

Bird also quickly established himself as the Celtics' leader. His scoring and passing skills, plus his all-out play, won over his teammates and the city of Boston almost instantly.

With Johnson leading the way, the Lakers won five NBA championships during the 1980s. Twice they beat the Celtics for the NBA crown. Magic was the league's Most Valuable Player (MVP) three times, and the playoffs MVP three times as well.

Larry Bird led the Celtics to three NBA championships during the 1980s, beating the Lakers once. He also won three league MVP awards, and won that award twice for the playoffs. He and the Celtics went head-to-head against Magic Johnson and the Lakers in 1984, 1985, and 1987. Those playoff games will go down as some of the greatest in the history of pro basketball.

Magic Johnson and Larry Bird were the two most dominant NBA players of the decade. Their careers will always be linked by a rivalry that began in college and continued for ten years in the pros. Together Bird and Johnson provided hundreds of memorable moments for basketball fans all over the country. ▪

The Lakers' Magic Johnson and the Celtics' Larry Bird battled each other in numerous memorable games during the decade.

When Pete Rose connected for this hit in 1985, he broke Ty Cobb's record for career hits. By the end of the decade, however, Rose had been forced out of baseball in disgrace.

The Rise and Fall of Charlie Hustle

Throughout his baseball career, Pete Rose often heard an umpire call, "You're out!" However, that call didn't prevent Rose from accumulating more base hits than anyone in baseball history. In 1989, however, Rose heard someone else call him out. Baseball Commissioner A. Bartlett Giamatti called Rose out of baseball for good. Rose was permanently banned from baseball for gambling on the game.

For nearly 25 years, Pete Rose had been one of the most popular and respected players in the game. In his home town of Cincinnati, he was a legend.

Rose began and ended his career in his home town. He was with Cincinnati the three times he won the National League Batting Championship. He helped lead the Reds to four National League pennants and two World Championships. And it was as a Cincinnati Red that Rose capped his long playing career by breaking one of baseball's most cherished records— Ty Cobb's career record of 4,191 base hits.

When Rose retired as a player, he stayed on as manager of the Reds. Though no one knew it at the time, becoming the Reds' manager was the beginning of the end for the baseball superstar.

Rose was a longtime gambler. Over the years he had made no secret of his fondness for betting at the racetrack. In the spring of 1989, he was charged with betting on baseball games. He denied the accusations.

"I'd be willing to bet you, if I was a betting man, that I have never bet on baseball," Rose answered jokingly. But the charges were no joke. If it was found that he had placed bets on other baseball teams, he could be suspended for a year. If he had bet on the Reds, his own team, he faced a lifetime suspension.

By the end of the summer, the evidence was in. The commissioner claimed he had proof that Rose had bet not only on baseball games, but on games played by his own team. Rose went down swinging, continuing to deny that he had bet on baseball.

Pete Rose had a lot to lose. He was forbidden from having any further contact with the game he had played for most of his adult life. In order to pay a gambling debt, he had sold the very bat he had swung for his record-breaking hit. Later, when he was found guilty of tax evasion, Rose even spent time in prison.

In 1992, Pete Rose would have been eligible for baseball's Hall of Fame. Before the betting scandal, his election was a sure thing. Now the Hall of Fame was another thing that Pete Rose had lost.

During his playing career, Pete Rose had been known as "Charlie Hustle." What he had lacked in raw talent, he had always made up for in hustle and drive. But Rose's drive to make a fast dollar hustled him right out of baseball. ■

49ers Strike Super Gold Four Times

"Team of the '80s," it said on the San Francisco 49ers' Super Bowl XXIII rings. No one could dispute that. The 'Niners had won three titles during the 1980s, and they put the frosting on the cake by winning Super Bowl XXIV in 1990.

It was a young San Francisco team that met the Cincinnati Bengals in Super Bowl XVI on January 24, 1982. The 49ers lineup included 20 new players. Quarterback Joe Montana was just a third-year player. But Bill Walsh used creativity and cunning to coach the team to a 26–21 victory over the Bengals. It was San Francisco's first National Football League championship. Just two years earlier, the 49ers had won only two games the entire season.

Montana captured the game's Most Valuable Player (MVP) award. However, it was the rebuilt San Francisco defense, led by four rookies in the backfield, that turned back the Bengal offense to clinch the game.

San Francisco's next Super Bowl appearance came in 1985, against the Miami Dolphins. The 49ers finished the regular season 15–1, setting a record for season wins. Despite this, Dolphins quarterback Dan Marino got most of the publicity going into the game. Although only a second-year player, Marino had had a record-breaking season in 1984. 'Niners quarterback Joe Montana was basically a quiet, modest guy who didn't seek attention.

Considering their season record, the 49ers felt they didn't get the respect they deserved. All that changed after the game,

which the 49ers won by a score of 38–16. Montana outplayed Marino from start to finish. He set Super Bowl records for passing yardage and rushing yardage by a quarterback. Once again, he was named the game's MVP.

The road to the 1989 Super Bowl was rougher for the 49ers. After a hard-fought 10–6 season, Montana showed his cool and his many skills in the conference championship game against the Chicago Bears. The wind-chill factor of 26 below zero in Chicago's Soldier Field didn't slow down the 49ers. They trounced the Bears, 28–3. The 49ers were on their way to another Super Bowl meeting with the Cincinnati Bengals.

Experts predicted that the 49ers would beat the Bengals easily, but it didn't happen that way. In fact, the 49ers were trailing 16–13, with just over three minutes left in the game. Then Montana took his team on one of its classic last-minute drives. They marched practically the length of the field. Then Montana hit John Taylor with a 10-yard bullet touchdown pass with just 34 seconds left. Final score: 49ers 20, Bengals 16.

The following year, the 49ers were back for Super Bowl XXIV. Under new coach George Seifert, they blew out the Denver Broncos 55–10. Montana was named Super Bowl MVP for the third time.

A decade of Super Bowls came to an end in that January 1990 game in New Orleans. After four championships, the "team of the '80s" still reigned supreme. ∎

San Francisco 49ers quarter-back Joe Montana led his team to four Super Bowl championships in nine years.

Spielberg and Lucas: Blockbuster Kings

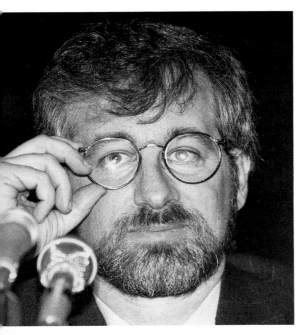

Alone—and together—Steven Spielberg (top) and George Lucas have created some of the most popular movies of all time.

He dropped in from "somewhere out there" and was left stranded on earth. He had a leathery face, a long neck, and a strange glowing finger. Despite all this—or because of it—the lovable character "E.T." took American movie audiences by storm during the summer of 1982.

The film *E.T. The Extra-Terrestrial* was directed by Steven Spielberg. It tells the story of a kindly being from outer space who crash-lands on earth and finds he has no way to return home. The alien is then befriended by earth children and hunted by evil government agents.

The movie went on to become the biggest moneymaker in Hollywood history. By the end of the decade, its ticket sales had topped $700 million worldwide.

Of course the fact that Steven Spielberg produced such a highly successful film really came as no surprise to anyone in Hollywood. Beginning in the mid-1970s, Spielberg has either produced or directed more movie blockbusters than anyone in film history. His string of hits over a 15-year period is nothing short of incredible: *Jaws* (1975); *Close Encounters of the Third Kind* (1977); *Raiders of the Lost Ark* (1981); *E.T.* (1982); *Poltergeist* (1982); *Indiana Jones and the Temple of Doom* (1984); *Back to the Future* (1985); and *Indiana Jones and the Lost Crusade* (1989).

In fact, the only Hollywood filmmaker to rival Spielberg's success is his close friend George Lucas. Lucas is the creator of the other major blockbuster series during the past 15 years—the original *Star Wars* (1977), and its two sequels, *The Empire Strikes Back* (1980) and *Return of the Jedi* (1983).

Spielberg and Lucas share much in common. Their films are filled with a sense of timeless fantasy, high adventure, and great special effects. The movies they've made reflect the admiration both of them have for the action-packed adventure films they grew up watching.

This feeling was best shown in the three movies the two men teamed up to make during the eighties: the Indiana Jones series. It was a series that Lucas conceived, produced, and helped write, and which Spielberg directed. The main character, Indiana Jones, is an archaeologist and adventurer played by Harrison Ford. Most movie fans took it for granted that Ford acted out on screen the adventures that Lucas and Spielberg had dreamed about in their youths.

E.T.'s ticket sales have topped $700 million worldwide.

Spielberg claims that "the only time I feel totally happy is when I'm watching films or making them." Then he must have been very happy during the 1980s. Breaking box office records time and again, both he and Lucas gave audiences what they wanted. Astounding special effects appealed to the eyes and the ears. Warmth and heroism appealed to the heart. And fantasy and adventure appealed to the spirit. Those were unbeatable combinations. ■

This Vincent van Gogh painting, *The Bridge at Trinquetaille*, sold for more than $20 million in 1987.

Art for Money's Sake

The High-Priced World of Art Collecting

Dutch painter Vincent van Gogh committed suicide in 1890 at the age of 37. He died a poor man, having sold only one of his paintings during his lifetime. On March 30, 1987, van Gogh's *Sunflowers*, painted in 1888, was sold at Christie's auction house in London. The price was $39.9 million. The amount was nearly *four times* the previous record for an auctioned painting. What's more, it was only the first of three van Gogh works that sold for multimillion dollar amounts during the same year.

In June, van Gogh's *The Bridge at Trinquetaille* sold for $20.2 million. The prices of the first two paintings seemed unbelievable until later that year. In November, van Gogh's *Irises*

sold for a whopping $53.9 million. The sale at Sotheby's auction house in New York City made front-page news all over the world.

The art market continued to boom during the late 1980s. In 1988, Pablo Picasso's *Acrobat and Young Harlequin* was sold for $38.5 million. One year later, Picasso's *Au Lapin Agile* sold for $40.7 million.

Contemporary art brought high prices, too. A 1959 painting by Jasper Johns claimed the record for the highest price paid for a work by a living artist. In 1988, Johns's painting *False Start* sold for $17 million. The painting had first sold in 1960 for just $3,150. Jasper Johns himself only received half that sum. Obviously it was neither

the artists nor their heirs who enjoyed the huge profits from the sales. The collectors were the ones who reaped rewards on their investments. The auction houses also made large commissions on the sales.

The skyrocketing prices were putting museums out of the market.

Who was actually buying art at these inflated prices during the 1980s? By 1988, the Japanese had become the major buyers, followed closely by the Europeans. Often Japanese companies, rather than individuals, were making the purchases. The Mitsukoshi department store paid the $38.5 million for Picasso's *Acrobat and Young Harlequin*. Yasuda Fire and Marine Insurance Company of Tokyo purchased van Gogh's *Sunflowers* for $39.9 million.

For most collectors, these works of art were investments. The value of many well-known paintings grew rapidly, often leaping millions of dollars in just a year. Also, many buyers believed that owning great art gave them importance. Other collectors valued art as timeless and universal. The beauty of a fine painting, some would say, is priceless.

Unfortunately, the skyrocketing price tags were putting museums out of the market. Many art lovers were sorry to see that happen. Once, great works of art could be seen by millions of people at exhibits all over the world. Now many were going to private collections to be enjoyed by a select few—until they were sold again for another record price. ∎

During the 1980s, Michael Jackson was one of MTV's most popular music video artists.

I Want My MTV!
Music Videos Change Pop Music

"**D**id you *see* that song?" many young people were asking during the 1980s. Music videos had added a new dimension to pop music. Fans not only listened to, but also looked at, their favorite songs.

Beginning in 1981, music videos came beaming into American homes over cable television's MTV (the Music Television channel). MTV showed popular recording artists performing their songs 24 hours a day, seven days a week. The music videos were usually interesting, often imaginative, and sometimes bizarre.

There are basically two types of music videos. Concert videos generally show a group or an artist performing. Concept videos are dramatic interpretations of a song.

Concept videos often tell a story. In *Thriller*, the video version of pop star Michael Jackson's hit song, a young woman's date becomes a nightmare. She watches, horrified, as her date (Jackson) grows fangs and sprouts body hair. A chorus line of ghouls joins her date-turned-monster in a frantic dance. The exciting production is like a mini-feature film. Produced at a cost of almost $1 million, *Thriller* became a landmark in music video history.

Rather than telling a story, some videos show images suggested by the song. A ship on the ocean becomes a race car, then a leopard, then a flaming guitar. Vivid images dissolve into one another or flash across the screen with lightning speed.

By 1984, MTV was bringing more than 300 videos a day into 22 million homes. Teenagers could drown themselves in the sights and sounds of pop music morning, noon, and night. That made some parents uneasy. They criticized the amount of violence shown in music videos. Women's groups complained that much of the violence was directed at women. They said many videos showed women in a sexist way.

At the beginning of the decade, MTV was criticized for ignoring minority performers. Most of MTV's early videos showed only white rock 'n' roll performers. In spite of a lack of video time, black artists gained in popularity. Rap—rhyming street talk with a heavy drum beat and a musical background—became the music that many fans wanted on MTV. By the end of the decade, minority artists had earned a much larger share of programming time.

Recording companies see music videos as a great way to promote their product and increase their sales. Air time on MTV can send a new song right to the top. Television programmers see videos as a means to attract advertisers. Hearing the ring of the cash register, more networks have added music videos to their programming. There is no doubt that music videos have changed popular music—and little doubt that they're here to stay. ∎

A Soviet Leader Who Changed the World

Mikhail Gorbachev might well be the most surprising government leader of the century. During the 1980s, Gorbachev unleashed an unexpected era of reform throughout the Communist world. He spurred new thinking and warmed relationships between nations. Mikhail Gorbachev quite simply changed the world forever.

Gorbachev was born to peasant parents in 1931 in a village near Stavropol in Russia. As a young man, he joined the Communist Youth League and moved up through the Communist Party. An honor student in high school, he was admitted to Moscow University law school.

Since the days of Josef Stalin, most Soviet leaders had been older men without a higher education. They kept themselves apart from the rest of the developed world. Gorbachev was different. He was a college graduate, and only 54 years old when he became the Soviet leader. And, unlike previous leaders, Gorbachev traveled widely. He was impressed by the progress he found outside the Soviet Union.

Shortly after he became Soviet leader in 1985, Gorbachev began to propose sweeping changes at home. His policy of *glasnost* (openness) called for less censorship in art, literature, and news reporting. *Perestroika* (restructuring) was another Gorbachev plan. It would re-organize the economy and re-duce government control of industry.

The economic overhaul would not be easy, Gorbachev warned. It would mean great sacrifices on the part of the Russian people. By the end of the decade, economic turmoil in the USSR would make Gorbachev more popular abroad than he was among his own people.

Gorbachev greatly improved Soviet relations with other nations. His travels won him unexpected popularity. When he visited Washington D.C. in 1987, he stepped out of his bullet-proof limousine and walked into a crowd. "I want to say hello!" he said warmly.

The world was surprised to find a Soviet leader so friendly and even humorous. But Gorbachev was also tough and very loyal to his homeland. Former Soviet foreign minister Andrei Gromyko said of Gorbachev, "This man has a nice smile, but he has iron teeth."

Although Gorbachev called for striking changes in his country, he was a dedicated Communist. But unlike previous Soviet leaders, he did not be-lieve that communism was bound to take over the world. "Surely, we can be competitors without being enemies," he said.

Gorbachev backed up his words not only with what he did, but with what he did not do. When Communist govern-ments in Eastern Europe began to fall, no Soviet tanks rolled in to keep them in power. Gorba-chev let freedom reign. By doing so, he led the way to a safer, more democratic world. ∎

Unlike past Soviet leaders, Mikhail Gorbachev often met with Soviet citizens to discuss their problems and concerns.

Jesse Jackson

Civil Rights Leader, Political Force

Many people said white America would never cast their votes for a black man for president. Jesse Jackson proved them wrong. On March 26, 1988, the 46-year-old Jackson became the first African-American to win a presidential primary election. Both black and white Democrats in Michigan chose him as their candidate. His victory proved that Americans can rise above racial prejudices. It also showed how far determination can take a poor boy from Greenville, South Carolina.

Jesse Louis Burns was born on October 8, 1941. His mother, Helen Burns, was an unmarried high-school student. When she married Charles Jackson, young Jesse took his stepfather's name. The family was poor, but they gave Jesse love and support.

Jackson quickly began to realize that things were not the same for blacks and whites in South Carolina. He had to walk five miles to an all-black school. Like other blacks in his town, he was not allowed to use drinking fountains and other facilities that were labeled "Whites Only."

An excellent student and athlete, Jackson accepted a football scholarship to the University of Illinois. He became disappointed that blacks couldn't play a more active role on campus. So he transferred to the all-black North Carolina Agricultural and Technical College. There he became a leader in the student movement for equal rights.

With a strong faith in God and a gift for public speaking, he decided to become a preach-

Jesse Jackson gives a "thumbs up" to his supporters in New York City during the 1988 presidential campaign.

er. After college he enrolled at the Chicago Theological Seminary.

In 1965, Jackson joined a civil rights march in Selma, Alabama. His eagerness impressed the leader of the march, Dr. Martin Luther King, Jr. Jackson left the seminary to head King's Chicago program, Operation Breadbasket. He organized boycotts against businesses in black neighborhoods that did not hire blacks.

In 1971, Jackson started his own organization, called PUSH (People United to Serve Humanity). He visited schools to talk about drug abuse and teen pregnancies.

Jesse Jackson made his first run for the presidency in 1984. He reached out not only to black voters, but to all who were poor and felt powerless.

He called his campaign the Rainbow Coalition because he hoped to represent people of all colors. Jackson received 3.3 million votes as a candidate for the Democratic presidential nomination in 1984. Most of his support came from the black community.

In 1988 Jackson ran for president again, this time winning 6.7 million Democratic votes. The Michigan primary showed that he could attract support outside the black community.

With his two tries for the presidency, Jesse Jackson had opened new doors of opportunity for minorities in America. As one black mother said, "Jesse Jackson may not ever become president of the United States. But he made it possible for my son to run . . . and win!" ∎

Margaret Thatcher

The Iron Lady Leads Great Britain

Margaret Thatcher didn't mind being known as the Iron Lady. In fact, she considered the nickname a compliment. It was iron will and steely self-confidence that won Thatcher three terms as Great Britain's prime minister.

She was born Margaret Hilda Roberts in the village of Grantham, England, in 1925. She first became interested in politics while studying at Oxford University. A strong conservative, she was president of Oxford's Conservative Association.

In 1951 Margaret married Denis Thatcher, a fellow conservative. He encouraged his wife's political ambitions.

Margaret was elected a member of Parliament from the Conservative Party in 1959. At age 34, she set off on the path that would lead to Number Ten Downing Street, the British "White House."

In 1975, the Conservatives elected Margaret Thatcher leader of their party. She was the first woman to hold that position. The Labor Party was in power, and as leader of the opposition party, Thatcher called for change. She criticized government ownership of business. Her policy, which became known as Thatcherism, stressed the importance of private enterprise.

By the late 1970s, Great Britain was going through very tough times. During a bitterly cold winter, labor strikes halted the delivery of oil. Trucks and trains stopped. Unheated schools were closed. On March 30, 1979, Margaret Thatcher called for a vote of no confidence in the Labor Party leadership. "The government has failed the nation," she declared. "It's time for it to go."

In May 1979, the Conservatives won a close election. Margaret Thatcher became the first woman prime minister of Great Britain.

To boost the economy, she announced lower income-tax rates. She cut social programs. Her critics called Thatcher cold-hearted toward the jobless and poor. In 1981, high unemployment brought riots throughout Great Britain. Thatcher responded with tougher police action rather than new job programs.

In 1983 Thatcher won a second term as prime minister. During the following years, she met frequently with U.S. President Ronald Reagan. The two leaders had much in common. Both were firmly anti-Communist, had pushed for increased defense spending, and followed conservative economic policies.

Thatcher also called on Mikhail Gorbachev, the Soviet Union's new leader. After lengthy talks, the two heads of state seemed to have formed the basis of a working relationship. Thatcher won new respect as a world leader.

In 1987, Britain held another national election. The Iron Lady was elected prime minister for a third term.

Margaret Thatcher had set out to play a leading role in her nation's political system. She was also determined to follow her own course of action and to stick to it despite heavy criticism. By the end of the 1980s, she had done both. ∎

Margaret Thatcher, Great Britain's first woman prime minister, was elected to that office three times.

OUR CENTURY: 1980-1990

GLOSSARY

AIDS: letters that stand for a fatal disease called Acquired Immune Deficiency Syndrome.

ANC: the African National Congress, a group fighting to end apartheid and racial discrimination in South Africa.

apartheid: a legally sanctioned system of extreme discrimination against black South Africans by the white minority rule.

assassination: the murder of a political leader or other important person.

civil war: a war between different groups of people within the same country.

Cold War: a war fought with words and propaganda between the governments of the United States and the Soviet Union after World War II.

glasnost: a Russian term for the new spirit of openness encouraged by Mikhail Gorbachev in the Soviet Union.

homeless shelters: places where people without homes can sleep and get a meal.

the "Iron Lady": a nickname for Britain's tough former prime minister, Margaret Thatcher.

landslide victory: a political victory in which the winner wins by a very large margin.

music videos: videos of popular music stars playing and performing their recordings, usually shown on television.

Muslims: people who follow a religion based on the teachings of their prophet, Mohammed.

PC: letters that stand for "personal computer."

resurgence: the re-emergence of something that had once been strong but then fell into the background.

Sandinistas: the organized popular movement that overthrew the dictatorship of Anastasio Somoza in Nicaragua. The group takes its name from a martyred freedom fighter, Sandino.

Solidarity: a workers' union that struck against the communist government of Poland and eventually caused its collapse.

special effects: simulations of fantastic or spectacular events in films, made possible by technology.

terrorists: people who commit acts of violence in order to try to achieve their political aims.

VCR: letters that stand for "video-cassette recorder," a machine that can be hooked up to a television to show film cassettes.

BOOKS FOR FURTHER READING

The titles listed below provide more detailed information about some of the people and events described in this book. Ask for them at your local library or bookstore.

George H. W. Bush: 41st President of the United States. Steffoff (Garrett Ed Corp)

Nelson Mandela: Speaking Out for Freedom in South Africa. Daniel and Pogrund (Gareth Stevens)

Portrait of a Decade: Nineteen-Eighties. Campling (Trafalgar Square)

Ronald W. Reagan, 40th President of the United States. Robbins (Garrett Ed Corp)

U.S.A. for Africa: Rock Aid in the 1980s. Berger (Franklin Watts)

The Year You Were Born, 1983. Martinet (Morrow & Co.)

PLACES TO WRITE AND VISIT

Communications Hall of Fame
72 Mountain Street
Sutton, Quebec J0E 2K0

National Air and Space Museum
Sixth Street & Independence Avenue
Washington, D.C. 20560

Smithsonian Institution
1000 Jefferson Drive S.W.
Washington, D.C. 20560

INDEX